Smith

THE BEST OF GRAND CANYON NATURE NOTES 1926–1935

THE BEST OF GRAND CANYON NATURE NOTES

1926–1935

EDITED
BY
Susan Lamb

GRAND CANYON NATURAL HISTORY ASSOCIATION
GRAND CANYON, ARIZONA

ISBN 0-938216-49-X
Library of Congress Card Catalog Number 94-075654

Designed by Christina Watkins

Illustrations, inspired by those in the original issues
of *Nature Notes*, by Tony Brown

Cover painting "Grand Canyon" by Gunnar Widforss,
courtesy of the Santa Fe Railway Collection of
Southwestern Art

Typography and production by TypeWorks
Lithography by Lorraine Press, Inc.

♻ Printed on recycled paper using vegetable-based inks

This book honors the
National Park Service ideals
of conservation and education,
and is dedicated to the park servants
who work toward achieving those goals.

CONTENTS

Introduction .... Page x

EXPLORING GRAND CANYON

CHAPTER I—Trails and Expeditions .... Page 2
Breaking a Trail Through Bright Angel Canyon—Our Sorrow—Scientific Work—Kaibab Trail—On Canyon Trails.

EARTH SCIENCE

CHAPTER II—The Canyon Itself .... Page 12
Theories Relating to Origin—EARTHQUAKE—What Causes the Canyon Walls to Recede?—The Origin of Bright Angel Canyon—A Lesson in Erosion—Landslides—Rock Slide in the Coconino Sandstone—Grand Canyon Minerals—Formations Exposed—Some Fucoids—Pages in Cambrian History—Crinoidal Limestone—The Flora of the Hermit Shale—Laoporus Goes Walking—A Probable Influence on Life in the Kaibab Sea—Remnants of the Age of Dinosaurs on South Rim—The Youthful Grand Canyon.

CHAPTER III—River, Sky, and Seasons .... Page 32
The Carrying Power of the Colorado River—The Colorado River—"The Explorer"—Frederick S. Dellenbaugh—Wind Rivers—The Blue Haze—Aurora Borealis—A Lunar Rainbow—A Siege of Fair Weather—Meteorological Data—Yavapai Catches a Bolt—Static Electricity—The Path of a Thunderstorm—Autumn—When Winter Comes—An Unseasonable Season—Spring is Near.

LIFE SCIENCE

CHAPTER IV—Life Zones, Plant Succession, and Flora .... Page 52

Environment—Irregularitics in Climatic-Belts—A Living Conquest—Mushrooms on the Kaibab—The Geaster—Broomrape—Mariposa Lily—Prince's Plume—Weeds—Canyon Rim Roses—Seeds—Sagebrush—The Yucca—A Food Plant of the Indians—Our Cactuses—Where Our Cacti Grow—Catsclaw—Pinyon Pine—Pinyon Pine Nuts—The 1933 "Pine Nut" Crop—Oh Cedar!—Western Yellow Pine (*Pinus ponderosa*)—Gambel Oaks—Quaking Aspen—Quaking Aspen: Its Future in the Park—Does Mistletoe Kill the Trees?

CHAPTER V—Invertebrates, Reptiles, Amphibians, and Fish .... Page 78

Some Beetles—An Interesting Bug—Cricket Notes—Dragonflies—Vandals of the Sand—The Polyphemus Moth—The Papilio Tribe—Scorpion Vs. Tarantula—Horned Toads—A "Reptile Story"—The Bluebellied Lizard—The Chuckwalla—Lizard Eat Lizard—The Grand Canyon Rattlesnake—Rattlesnakes on the Canyon Rim—A Gopher-Snake Lunches—Amphibians—Trout Propagation—Planting Fish Eggs.

CHAPTER VI—Birds .... Page 96

Water Ouzel—Redshafted Flicker—Avian Cliff-Dwellers—Birding—The Turkey Buzzard—The Gathering of the Jay Clan—The Hermit of Horn Creek—A Winter Resident—Crossbill—Bird Migration Dates—Junco Visits Both Rims—Some Wildlife Observations.

CHAPTER VII—Mammals .... Page 110

Champion Barker—Pocket Mice—Button, Button, Who Has the Button?—A Curious Collection—Kaibab Squirrel; Abert

Squirrel—Dining Solitaire—Notes on Porcupines—The Sonora Beaver—The Raccoon of Havasupai—Ringtailed Cats—The Common Skunk—The Badger and Its Environment—Lady Hecate—A Bitter Struggle—A Near Tragedy—Kaibab Deer . . . On South Rim—Flying Deer—A Unique Combination—Bucks Grow Bold—Deer Antlers—Antlers as an Age Indicator—Hermit Steer—Wild Burros—Status of the Desert Bighorn—Mountain Sheep Observed—An Experimental Repair Job—The American Pronghorn—A Coyote Tale—Fox Holds Up Party—Bare Facts About Bear Tracks—Cougars on the South Rim.

HUMAN HISTORY

CHAPTER VIII—Archaeology and Ethnobotany .... Page 146
Wayside Museum—Grand Canyon Archaeology—A Large Cliff Dwelling—Ancient Pottery Rebuilt—Indian Uses of Juniper—A Food Plant of the Indians—The Yucca—Some Grand Canyon Plants and Their Uses.

CHAPTER IX—History .... Page 160
The Naming of the Grand Canyon—The Coronado Expedition—How Pipe Creek Received Its Name—History Note—Widforss—Yavapai Observation Station—The Reference Library—Grand Canyon Natural History Association—A National Park Creed.

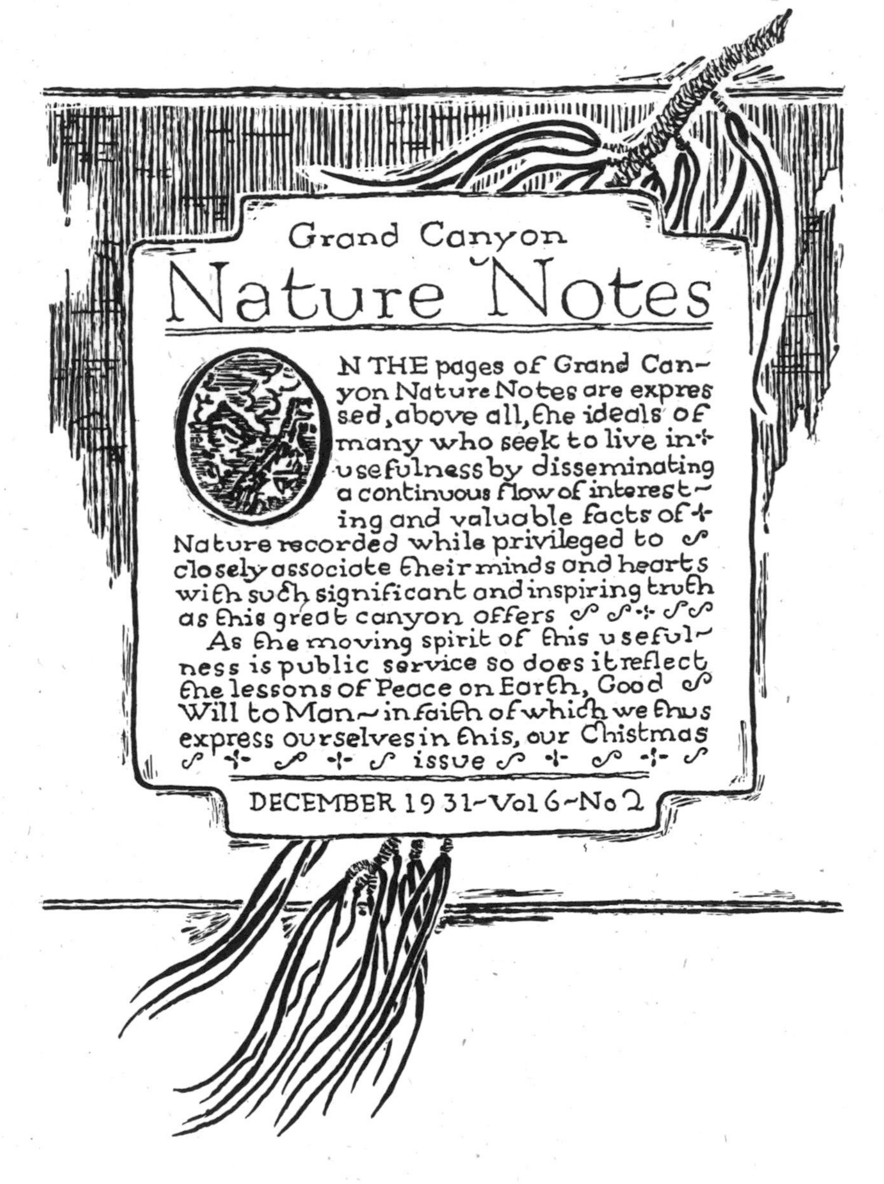

Grand Canyon

Nature Notes

ON THE pages of Grand Canyon Nature Notes are expressed, above all, the ideals of many who seek to live in usefulness by disseminating a continuous flow of interesting and valuable facts of Nature recorded while privileged to closely associate their minds and hearts with such significant and inspiring truth as this great canyon offers.

As the moving spirit of this usefulness is public service so does it reflect the lessons of Peace on Earth, Good Will to Man—in faith of which we thus express ourselves in this, our Chistmas issue

DECEMBER 1931—Vol 6—No 2

INTRODUCTION

From 1926 until 1935, Grand Canyon National Park printed monthly collections of reports and essays called *Nature Notes*. A diverse group of people—naturalists, visiting scientists, and even a park superintendent inspired by a moonlit walk—contributed anecdotes, observations, and musings about the natural world to more than one hundred issues of the *Notes*, which were then distributed to the public free of charge.

Nature Notes reveal how some unusual people saw an extraordinary place. They wrote as the inspiration struck them, in language that can be funny but is more often lyrical and even reverent. It is always vivid: ant lions are "Vandals of the Sand" and mistletoe is a "brigand" with "degenerate little roots."

These writers established a tradition of dedication to the Grand Canyon that has endured for generations. They identified the main themes that are still interpreted for Canyon visitors today. Although we have learned a great deal more and refined our answers somewhat, the basic questions endure: How was the Canyon formed? What is the river like? What kind of animals live here? How does the climate affect everything?

When Grand Canyon National Park was established in 1919, park rangers were modestly-educated generalists responsible for the wellbeing rather than the enlightenment of visitors to the park. Along with many other duties, Grand Canyon's four rangers patrolled the rims and inner canyon to help the lost or injured, served as policemen, and fought forest fires. But such was the enthusiasm of these early rangers that within a few years, they also found time to staff an "Information Room" for the park's visitors, who numbered about fifty thousand annually.

The Information Room—a combination of library, species collection, and visitor center—opened with the help of private funds in 1921. Grand Canyon's educational offerings expanded quickly after that, as an ever-increasing number of visitors asked about the geology, flora and fauna, and human story of the Canyon. Although all employees were still expected to perform general duties when necessary, the park hired Glen Sturdevant, an Army veteran with a degree in geology from the University of Arizona, to offer nature walks and campfire programs in the summer of 1925. Sturdevant's programs were so successful that the park hired him full-time the following year to develop an *interpretive* (educational) program for park visitors.

One of Sturdevant's first steps was to launch *Nature Notes*. He solicited articles from everyone associated with Grand

Canyon at the time, including illustrious scientists, park administrators, and his wife, Eileen (who wrote charming stories about her household's many furred and feathered guests). Sturdevant himself wrote about lots of things: birds, skunks, trees, roses, and of course, rocks.

Altogether, a handful of naturalists wrote well over half of the essays published. Through their writings, we come to know quite a bit about them. Edwin Dinwiddie McKee, who replaced Glen Sturdevant in 1929 and served as park naturalist until 1940, was the most prolific. McKee was an intensely observant man, a talented teacher and scholar who greeted every day with enthusiasm. He led nature walks for the general public, wrote more *Nature Notes* than anybody else on a vast array of topics, and corresponded with noted scientists, all the while conducting field research leading to his own doctorate in geology. Soon after succeeding Sturdevant, McKee married another Grand Canyon naturalist, Barbara Hastings, who also wrote articles on many subjects for *Nature Notes*.

PARK NATURALIST EDWIN MCKEE

Donald McHenry and Earl Count presented geology talks at Yavapai Observation Station. They did not confine their essays to geology, however, but contributed many lively articles about the Canyon's trails, weather, birds, and lizards. Others focussed more narrowly. Clyde Searl was particularly intrigued by insects. Botanist Pauline Mead described the life cycles of countless species of plants. P.P. (Preston) Patraw, the park's assistant superintendent, usually wrote about management problems. However, the spring he married Pauline Mead,

Patraw was inspired to offer the following:

OBSERVATION

ALONG THE HERMIT RIM ROAD, South Rim, the cliffrose (*Cowania stansburiana*) [now *Purshia stansburiana*] is now blooming in exceptional profusion where there is sunlight. In the shade, green buds only are seen. Many bushes are so covered with blossoms that the whole effect is that of a mass of plumes.

Although Grand Canyon received two hundred thousand visitors a year by 1929, those who lived there led an isolated existence, particularly in the winter. Apart from bridge games, a local rodeo, and occasional trips to town, there were few amusements available for them. Yet these people clearly considered themselves lucky. They were enthralled with the natural world, and their fascination is contagious.

BOTANIST PAULINE PATRAW

We hold our breath as Eddie McKee scoops a feisty little bat out of a pond. We watch Polly Mead energetically digging up a mysterious plant to learn how and why it grows where it does. And we can hardly wait to go take a look ourselves—at the rocks, the birds, and whatever else may be out there.

By far the most popular topic of the early naturalists was animal behavior. They loved to make pets of the wildlife, a practise frowned upon today because of the dire consequences for both captive and keeper.

The documentation of such early policies and conditions

makes these *Nature Notes* a valuable reference in understanding today's management of Grand Canyon resources. For example, the park no longer issues birdfeed to its resident staff because, as we read in these pages, naturalists observed that many birds were so dependent on this food that they failed to make their annual migrations. We find the roots of a persistent environmental problem here in accounts of the Kaibab deer herd, which increased in number exponentially after the extermination of mountain lions on the North Rim.

Fires are now managed rather than suppressed entirely as they were for years, in the hope of restoring a more natural and healthy condition to the forest. Camping in the middle of archaeological sites is forbidden, no matter how well they may serve as windbreaks!

The Grand Canyon Natural History Association took over publication of *Nature Notes* in 1931. As the years went by, however, more educational programs and publications developed, and the *Notes* were discontinued. This re-publication of excerpts from *Nature Notes* is again sponsored by the Grand Canyon Natural History Association, to commemorate the seventy-fifth anniversary of the establishment of Grand Canyon National Park.

About one-eighth of hundreds of entries are included in this collection, arranged by subject in roughly the same proportion as in the complete *Nature Notes*. In their original, mimeographed form, the Nature Notes are dotted with typographical and grammatical errors, digressions, and the occasional wild conjecture. The notes have been lightly edited here, but most of their delightful quirkiness remains.

U.S. DEPARTMENT OF THE INTERIOR

NATIONAL PARK SERVICE
GRAND CANYON NATIONAL PARK

Vols. 1–9 Nos. 1–12
GRAND CANYON NATURE NOTES March, 1926–March, 1935.

This bulletin is issued monthly for the purpose of giving information to those interested in the natural history and scientific features of the Grand Canyon National Park. Additional copies of these bulletins may be obtained free of charge by those who can make use of them, by addressing the Superintendent, Grand Canyon National Park, Grand Canyon, Arizona.

EDUCATIONAL PLANS

E.T. Scoyen, Chief Park Ranger
April, 1926.

THE EDUCATIONAL WORK of the National Park Service should not be confused with the publicity and propaganda work that usually masquerades under this heading. The parks are great wilderness areas which are to be forever preserved in their natural state. They have been called outdoor museums, and are places where the wonders of the great American out-of-doors are preserved, not behind plate glass, but as geologists often say: "in place." Here the nature lover can study nature as it has always been. It is with the intention of having all people appreciate these facts, and to enable them to interpret the great lessons of nature and life, that the educational work in the National Park is undertaken.

Plans for the educational work in Grand Canyon National Park the coming summer include the regular issue of these *Nature Notes*, nature guide trips, campfire lectures, and museum service.

During the course of the next few years, this little bulletin will cover practically all the outdoor features of the park, such as the flora, fauna, and natural phenomena. If anyone receiving these bulletins will preserve them carefully, in a few years he will have a fine library on the natural history. . . .

All of these activities should greatly stimulate interest in the park and the nature features therein. It should benefit the visitor to be able to understand the things he sees around him.

Although the beginning will be modest, we hope to make it a feature of each person's visit to the Grand Canyon National Park in the near future.

EXPLORING GRAND CANYON

CHAPTER I
Trails and Expeditions

Crossing the Dangerous Colorado River
Posed a Major Challenge to Surveying the Grand Canyon.

BREAKING A TRAIL THROUGH BRIGHT ANGEL CANYON

Francois Matthes, U.S. Geological Survey
November, 1927.

IN THE SPRING OF 1902, it was my privilege to be assigned to the task of beginning the topographic mapping of the Grand Canyon for the U.S. Geological Survey. . . . But at that time there was no trail across from rim to rim, nor was there a bridge over the Colorado. We found ourselves face to face with a barrier more formidable than the Rocky Mountains: an abyss two hundred and eighty miles long containing an unbridged, unfordable, dangerous river. . . .

About the middle of August, when the river had subsided to a moderate level, we set out with a pack train of ten animals. W.W. Bass kindly consented to our using his home-made boat. . . .

The camp equipment was quickly ferried over, but the . . . animals, worn out by the heat, and unnerved by their descent over the great rockslide at the foot of the trail, could not be induced to enter the water. . . . They were led down to a rock platform, ostensibly so they might quench their thirst, then suddenly they were pushed over into the swirling flood. Quickly behind the boat they were then towed across, one by one, but in their frenzy many of them tried to swim back, or downstream, or even to climb into the boat, so that the rowers were more than once in danger of being dragged down over the turbulent rapids below the crossing. Eventually, however, all the animals were landed safely on the north side. . . .

As autumn set in, and the prospect of a snowstorm grew more and more imminent . . . we were forced to consider a retreat to the south side. The survey by that time had progressed as far east as the head of Bright Angel Canyon. . . .

Now, Bright Angel Canyon is carved along a great fracture in the earth's crust. . . . It did not take us long, therefore, to discover a route along this fault where the Redwall, the cliff of the Coconino sandstone, and the lesser cliffs are interrupted by slopes of debris. . . .

On the 7th of November, when heavy clouds presaged a change in the weather, we hastily broke camp and proceeded down our new trail. So steep was it in certain places that the animals fairly slid down on their haunches. So narrow between the rocks was it at one point, that the larger packs could not pass through and had to be unloaded. Of accidents there were more than can here be chronicled, but none of them, fortunately, was of a serious nature. The mule carrying the most precious burden—the instruments and the newly made maps—was led with particular care, but she lived up to her reputation and made the trip without a stumble. . . .

SURVEY PARTY AT CAPE ROYAL

After a sojourn of several days in Bright Angel Canyon, during which the course of the stream was duly mapped, we proceeded to the river and once more faced the problem of crossing it. With the aid of a boat lent by a friendly prospector, however, this was accomplished with little difficulty; the animals, now homeward bound, having apparently lost their fear of the river. Soon, therefore, we were scrambling up the prospector's steep burro trail, and without serious mishap reached our goal on the South Rim.

OUR SORROW

M.R. Tillotson, Superintendent
February, 1929.

FRIENDS OF THE NATIONAL PARK SERVICE and of Grand Canyon National Park will be shocked and grieved to learn of the untimely death by drowning of Glen E. Sturdevant, Park Naturalist, and Fred Johnson, Park Ranger. This irretrievable loss occurred on the morning of February 20, when in company with Chief Ranger James P. Brooks, Sturdevant and Johnson were returning from a ten-day trip in the Canyon, the object of which was the collection of specimens of scientific interest, securing data on Canyon flora and fauna, search for prehistoric ruins and other objects of archaeological interest, as well as a general exploration of some of the unknown regions of the Canyon.

While breaking camp that morning, the boys had been congratulating themselves on the fact that, although they had been in some rather dangerous places, the trip had been completed without the slightest accident and they now had only to go on out, the expectation being that they would reach home that afternoon. In crossing the Colorado River however, their boat was caught in an eddy, and Johnson was thrown into the water. Brooks immediately jumped overboard to his rescue, but failed to reach him and was himself swept downstream into the rapids. In the meantime, the boat containing Sturdevant was also caught in the rapids, and Brooks in the water, most of the time being drawn below the surface by the undercurrent, saw no more of him. How Brooks ever escaped he does not know, but he finally found himself cast ashore more dead than alive. . . .

Glen was laid to rest in the village cemetery, alongside the Grand Canyon he loved so well and for the cause of which he gave his life. Fred still sleeps in the Canyon itself, and a more fitting grave no National Park officer could have. . . . Just as truly as if they had fallen on the field of battle, these brave men laid down their lives in the service of their country. Their lives, their work, and their death will always be an encouragement and an inspiration to those of us who are left to carry on. May we not fail them.

Glen Sturdevant was Grand Canyon's first Park Naturalist. Although a graduate of the University of Arizona in geology, Glen Sturdevant was a generalist at heart. He launched the *Nature Notes*, and often contributed to them on a variety of topics.

SCIENTIFIC WORK

June, 1929.

GRAND CANYON NATIONAL PARK has been fortunate in having several of the country's leading scientists numbered among its visitors this past month.

Dr. David White, principal geologist U.S. Geological Survey, has spent some three weeks in a study of the fossil flora of the region, collecting and studying the plants along all of the principal Canyon trails. . . .

Dr. H.C. Bryant of the California Fish and Game Commission arrived on the North Rim on June 10, and three days later on the South Rim, to make a special study of the biological problems of the park. . . .

On June 10, Dr. J.P. Buwalda of the California Institute of Technology arrived for a short visit during which time he made a study of the geology, especially in its relation to the educational program at Grand Canyon.

Dr. John C. Merriam, President of the Carnegie Institution, spent five days examining questions relative to the practical administration of the educational program, and to the presentation to the public of the scientific story of Grand Canyon.

Mr. Vernon Bailey of the U.S. Biological Survey has been continuing his work in the Grand Canyon region with considerable success. . . .

The two Ranger Naturalists arrived about the middle of the month to take up their scientific duties and educational duties for the summer. Mr. Stephen B. Jones, formerly of the University of Washington and also Harvard University, is stationed

---

Grand Canyon has always drawn scholars and scientists from many different specialties. Their studies and publications add immeasurably to our understanding of the Canyon. Dr. David White published "Flora of the Hermit Shale, Grand Canyon, Arizona" through the Carnegie Institution in December of 1929. In 1935, Vernon Bailey authored "Mammals of the Grand Canyon," the first in a series of scientific bulletins issued by the Grand Canyon Natural History Association. In addition, seasonal park naturalists have contributed thousands of valuable observations and specimens to the park's collections over the years.

on the North Rim, and Mr. Earl W. Count of the State Teachers College, San Jose, California, is located on the South Rim.

VERNON BAILEY'S U.S. GEOLOGICAL SURVEY CAMP
AT PIPE CREEK, 1929.

KAIBAB TRAIL

Earl W. Count, Ranger Naturalist
June, 1930.

TO KNOW THE CANYON, go down into it. That adage holds good, no matter how much one may skirt the rim. The newest trail leads from Yaki Point down onto the Tonto Platform, where it meets the trail descending and crossing the river to the mouth of Bright Angel Creek. To tramp this trail when the morning opens briskly, just to tramp, with no ulterior motive, is one way to keep from growing old. . . .

The trail is broad and well-marked, and covered with the deep dust of the formations it crosses. You can tell roughly by the color of the trail when you have finished the whitish-pink Coconino Sandstone and have struck the red Hermit Shale. . . .

INTO THE CANYON ON THE BRIGHT ANGEL TRAIL.

Coconino Sandstone and have struck the red Hermit Shale. . . .

The battlements that you once looked down upon grow and grow and grow until they solemnly stare high over your head, as sublimely unmindful of your puny presence as when you were above them. And you have the humble yet exhilarating experience of feeling lost and glad of it.

Down you go, and out onto a long spur of Supai Sandstone, where a sparse forest of agaves point their flowered poles above a low, bristling crown of spiky leaves. And here it comes upon you as though you had never thought of it before: the Canyon is BIG. The citadels, the buttresses have retreated behind you; others ahead are bigger without apparently coming closer; and you are rejoiced at the open desolation and the protean solitude. Then it strikes as fitting that the world was not made for men, but rather man for the world. Perhaps an alert little lizard scurries off, then stops to view you inquisitively. He is simply another creature, and so are you, and you are glad of the kinship.

ON CANYON TRAILS, PARTS I AND II

Edwin D. McKee, Park Naturalist
August and September, 1933.

UNDOUBTEDLY, THE BEST KNOWN of Grand Canyon trails is the Bright Angel, which starts at Grand Canyon Village, and descending the great valley caused by a fault of the same name, passes through Indian Gardens, and thence on to the Colorado River below. . . . During part of the past century, and perhaps for a long time before, the natural route which the trail now follows was used by Havasupai Indians who lived and farmed at Indian Gardens. . . .

Today the Kaibab Trail, the construction of which was completed by the National Park Service in 1928, is the only practical route for crossing from rim to rim of Grand Canyon. Large parts of it, particularly on the south side of the Colorado River, were built by the sheer power of blasting. . . .

. . . [T]he Tanner Trail was used by the Navajo Indians under Old Begonia when they were trying to escape the American soldiers under Colonel Kit Carson in the 'sixties. . . . Although today this remote section is seldom frequented by man, there are many evidences of his former presence. Rock piles and cairns are to be seen in numerous places, and even an ancient distillery was found near the upper part of Chuar Creek. According to many stories that still survive, this section of Grand Canyon was a favorite hideout for renegades, poachers, and horse thieves.

West of the Tanner Trail is the Hance Trail, or what still remains of it, leading down Red Canyon to the river . . . it is a reworked Indian trail and was traveled in February 1882 by a Mrs. Edward Ayres, who was reputed to be the first white woman to go to the bottom of the Grand Canyon. Later, it was used to some extent for packing asbestos out of the Canyon from mines located across the river. . . .

The trail below Grandview was formerly known as the Berry Trail, after the late Mr. P.D. Berry who built it. Within recent years, however, it has commonly been called the Grandview Trail. . . . The primary purpose in building it was to enable the working of copper mines near its lower end.

THE NAME "HERMIT," which has been given to numerous objects located in the area just west of Grand Canyon Village, was originally suggested by the presence in that region of a pioneer named Louie Boucher.

What is probably the most seldom traveled and least known Canyon trail today was built by old Louie sometime between 1889 and 1893. The upper part leads to the charming locality known as Dripping Springs, entering Hermit Basin from the southwest. A continuation of it along the upper west walls of Hermit Canyon descends into Boucher Canyon farther down, and there Louie established what must have been a rather comfortable if isolated camp.

. . . [T]he Topocoba, which starts near a spring having the same name . . . leads to the Indian village of Supai down in Havasu Canyon.

The old Bass Trail, descending from a place near Havasupai Point down Bass Canyon . . . was largely developed by the famous pioneer W.W. Bass, recently deceased. The section leading from the South Rim to the Red Esplanade shelf below probably started as an Indian trail, for it was used by the Havasupais to Mystic Springs at the base of Mt. Huethawali many years ago. Sometime in the [18-] '90s, that spring is reported to have disappeared following an earthquake. . . .

In later years, Bass himself developed both copper and asbestos mines in the area and used his trail to the South Rim in packing out these minerals. He also built up a good tourist trade, and in 1900 developed a fine fruit orchard and garden plot near the mouth of Shinumo Creek.

EARTH SCIENCE

CHAPTER II
The Canyon Itself

THEORIES RELATING TO ORIGIN OF THE CANYON

Glen E. Sturdevant, Park Naturalist
March, 1927.

UPON VIEWING ONE OF THE MAJOR WORKS of nature such as the Grand Canyon of Arizona, the question: "How was it formed?" presents itself to the onlooker. That the human mind is ever seeking to explain the seemingly un-real of the realities of nature is evidenced by the theories advanced for the presence of such a mighty chasm. . . .

From the numerous theories, it is seen that many persons are prone to explain any of the major works of nature, especially those on the magnitude and scale of the Grand Canyon, as being made by some cataclysm, or great convulsion of nature. In general, the element of time is neglected in the explanation. Minutes, rather than millions of years, are used as a working criterion. No undue amount of violence such as earthquake, volcanism, or flood made the Grand Canyon area untenantable while the masterpiece was being carved. Earthquakes undoubtedly occurred at infrequent intervals during the uplift of the region. [But] the same beds of sedimentary rocks, present on both sides of the river, appear remarkably horizontal, dipping very gently to the southwest about one hundred feet to the mile.

The accepted theory governing the origin of the Grand Canyon is erosion in all of its phases, such as wind, rain, heat, cold, and running water.

EARTHQUAKE GRAND CANYON

Donald E. McHenry, Junior Park Naturalist
February, 1935.

OF THE THREE MOST POPULAR misconceptions about the origin of the Grand Canyon, one is the belief that the canyon is the result of a tremendous earthquake some time way back in the dim, distant, long ago. Geologists today recognize no evidence to justify any such theory. . . .

Although this earthquake theory exists only in the minds of the uninformed, it is nevertheless a fact that earthquakes do sometimes happen in the Grand Canyon. . . .

The writer was resting quietly at home at 7:00 P.M. Mountain Standard Time of January 4th, when he was aroused by what seemed to be someone shaking the door. When he investigated, much to his surprise he found no one there. . . .

Not until the entire Grand Canyon Village population was startled by an unmistakable shock at 9:25 P.M., did it occur to the writer that the experience of two-and-a-half hours earlier was the result of earth tremors. The quake of 9:25 P.M. was quite convincing, lasting for about one minute. It showed itself in the form of a rolling, wavelike motion, and was active enough to set dishes dancing. This

Earthquakes were more of a mystery in Donald McHenry's day. Geologists now believe that quakes in the Grand Canyon area occur as the earth's crust is "extended," or stretched here. In 1959, the strongest Arizona earthquake to be recorded by instruments struck Fredonia, only about ninety miles north of the Canyon, with a magnitude of 5.5. 1992 was particularly active, with a "swarm" of sixty-eight earthquakes measuring up to 4.5. Another rough jolt came on April 29, 1993, with a magnitude 5.4 temblor centered about thirty miles south of the Canyon.

disturbance was accompanied by distinct subterranean rumblings, which several people thought proceeded from south to north. People at Phantom Ranch in the bottom of the Canyon reported the tremors quite disturbing and the accompanying noise decidedly noticeable. Other shocks occurred at 10:40 the same evening and at 4:30 A.M., January 5th.

The most severe shock of the series came at 1:10 A.M., January 10th. This awakened sleepers with a start, causing many to jump out of bed in alarm. Joe Brown, caretaker for the Union Pacific hotel at Bright Angel Point on the North Rim, landed on the floor, gun in hand, ready for the intruder whom he supposed was banging at his cabin door. . . .

People at Phantom Ranch were vigorously jolted. Some of the C.C.C. boys stationed near Phantom Ranch were so scared that they wanted to leave the area immediately. Their fear was quieted only after some persuasion from their superiors. Ed Laws, at Indian Gardens down in the Canyon, reported very noticeable activity at that place accompanied by some minor rock slides, all from the western wall of this valley. . . .

WHAT CAUSES THE CANYON WALLS TO RECEDE?

Glen E. Sturdevant, Park Naturalist
September, 1928.

AS ONE VIEWS THE GRAND CANYON—the grandest of all canyons—he is invariably impressed with its magnitude. From rim to rim, it varies in width from four to eighteen miles. From the rims the great transporting agent—the Colorado River—appears like a narrow ribbon winding its way through a small, tortuous, inner canyon scarcely four hundred feet wide at its depths. To the layman, it is a puzzling situation to analyze: a river cutting a path three to four hundred feet wide, while the rims above vary in width from four to eighteen miles. He concludes, therefore, that the river must have been eighteen miles wide at one time, in order to leave a canyon of that width at the widest place. The causes, however, of the great width of the Grand Canyon at the rims as compared to the relatively narrow channel, are due to various reasons other than the Colorado. Chief among those factors causing the recession of the Canyon walls might be listed: vegetation, changes in temperature, wind, rain, running water, chemical action, faulting, and gravity. These various factors are really interdependent in accomplishing the recession of the cliffs.

THE ORIGIN OF BRIGHT ANGEL CANYON

Edwin D. McKee, Park Naturalist
December, 1931.

THE LENGTH, DEPTH, AND STRAIGHTNESS of the tributary canyon through which flows Bright Angel

Creek make that gorge one of the outstanding and most striking features of the central Grand Canyon area. Nor have its dimensions and shape become emphasized to such an extent by mere accident. On the contrary, they are the result of a great fault or break in the earth's crust, which occurred not far back in geological history. The rocks to the west of Bright Angel Creek were raised with respect to those to the east, as can be seen in the present upper levels of the canyon sides. This particular break—resulting from crustal movement—from the vertical slipping of one rock mass past another—is known as the Bright Angel fault. . . .

Rock layers were so broken and shattered along its eighteen-mile length that streams and running water found a comparatively easy task in cutting into them, and thereby excavating the canyon mentioned. The influence of the Bright Angel fault in shaping this part of the Grand Canyon, therefore, has been tremendous.

A LESSON IN EROSION

A. Russell Croft, Ranger Naturalist
August, 1932.

ON FRIDAY, JULY 8TH, NATURE PROVIDED an excellent demonstration of the effectiveness of a heavy rain in eroding the walls of Grand Canyon. At that time, about twenty-five people were in the vicinity of Yavapai Observation Station when a storm broke. All the adjectives usually applied to a raging rain could have been used in that case without danger of exaggeration. The rain came down "in sheets—in bucketsfull."

Beyond the large west window at the Observation Station, this somewhat rare demonstration of erosion was being staged by the forces of nature—the same forces that have been operative in eroding the canyon walls for vast numbers of years. The crowd watched, first in silence and then with mild exclamations of astonishment. The canyonside, as far as visible, was literally a sheet of water. The water was thick with sand and mud, and rocks of considerable size were being moved downward by its force. The entire surface seemed to be moving toward the canyon bottom.

The storm raged for twenty minutes and when it lifted, every side canyon and depression contained a stream of liquid mud. . . . A few thousand more tons of sediment had been started towards the flood plain of the Colorado, and a small group of tourists had received an excellent lesson in erosion.

LANDSLIDES AND THEIR PART IN WIDENING THE GRAND CANYON

Edwin D. McKee, Park Naturalist
June, 1933.

AN IMPORTANT COROLLARY OF RUNNING WATER as an erosive agent is seen in the work of gravity, as exemplified by landslides. Although undoubtedly assisted and affected by numerous other forces, the start of most recent slides within the Grand Canyon can be traced either to the direct or to the indirect action of water. To be sure, the usual results of water work are found at the base of every major cliff in the form of talus slopes, but examples of definite slides from this cause are also numerous. . . .

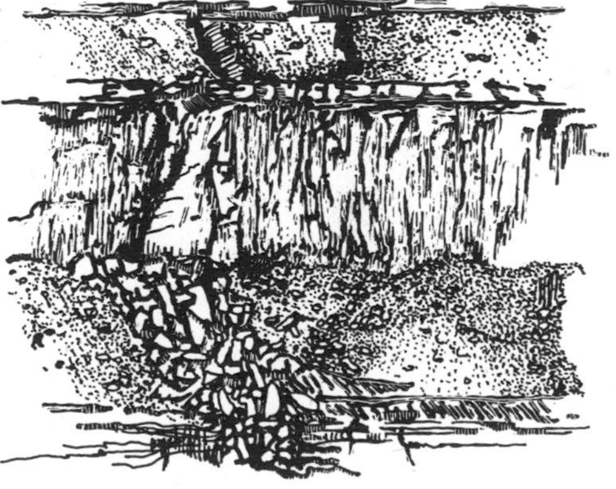

Rockslide in the Redwall

So far as can be determined, these falling rocks are usually sections of great cliffs, from beneath which soft shales have been undermined. In the nearly horizontal strata of the Canyon walls, vertical joints seem to have much influence on slides. In about twenty records examined, it was also found that most of the movements occurred during thaws following winter snows, although many had been caused directly by summer cloudbursts.

ROCK SLIDE IN THE COCONINO SANDSTONE

Russell Grater and Harold H. Hawkins,
Ranger Naturalists
January, 1935.

ON AUGUST 13TH ABOUT ELEVEN O'CLOCK in the morning, a sudden roar and a trembling of the foundations of Yavapai Observation Station on the South Rim advertised the presence of a rock slide below. A few seconds later, dust began rising in vast quantities on the Canyon side of the station—first white, then changing with astonishing rapidity to cream color, and then red. For about a minute and a half, the Canyon was almost completely obscured by the rising cloud of dust. Gradually, however, the air became clear again, but a heavy layer of dust over the glass cases and chairs in the station remained as witness to the event.

An examination of the walls beneath the station revealed that a column of rock approximately one hundred fifty feet high, twenty feet wide, and six feet thick had collapsed in the lower half of the Coconino formation.

The entire display was very spectacular while it lasted, and produced an extreme case of "nerves" among many of the Yavapai visitors who were present.

A SUMMARY OF GRAND CANYON MINERALS

Hugh H. Waesche, Ranger Naturalist
August, 1932.

THE MOST IMPORTANT of the three great minerals of Grand Canyon is quartz, which is the chief constituent of most sandstones. Sand grains which form them are derived usually from previously crystallized quartz of igneous origin. Also, primary crystalline quartz deposited from solution is quite common in cavities in the various Grand Canyon formations. Quartz is, as almost everyone knows, silicon dioxide. It is the most plentiful mineral in the earth's crust.

Second most abundant is calcium carbonate, which is deposited from water solutions. . . . If crystalline, it is known as calcite (rocks composed of crystalline calcite are called marbles), but if not crystalline, it forms limestones which are chemically similar. . . .

The third major sedimentary mineral is kaolin, which makes up a high percentage of the material composing the shales or mud formations of Grand Canyon as elsewhere. Shales are derived from rocks which, on weathering, have altered to kaolin. Kaolin is a hydrous aluminum silicate [one of the common clay minerals].

Minor minerals found in the sedimentary rocks of the region are: iron oxides, manganese oxides, barite, copper, lead, etc. The common forms of iron are hematite and limonite. It is these minerals which give the familiar red and yellow colors to so many of the formations. Hematite or limonite, along with calcite, are often the cementing materials which hold together the sand grains of a sandstone.

FORMATIONS EXPOSED AT THE GRAND CANYON

Glen E. Sturdevant, Park Naturalist
July, 1927.

THE OLDEST ROCKS . . . are composed of crystalline schists, gneisses, and granitic rocks of Archean age [see note below]. . . . These rocks form the walls of the Inner Granite Gorge. . . . All of the types of rocks that make up the Archean series are hard and equally resistant to erosion, thereby giving a sharp, ragged, V-shaped profile to the Inner

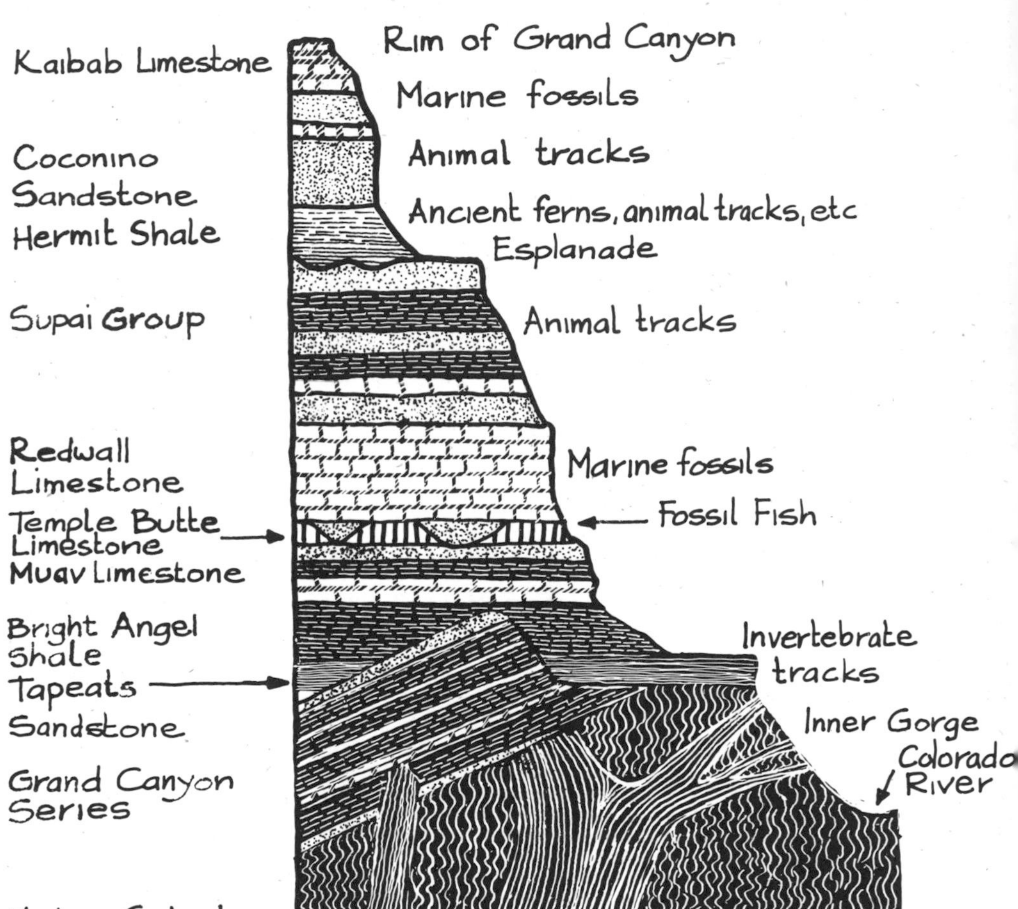

Gorge. By their darker color, crystalline character, ragged profile, and lack of stratification, they are easily distinguished from the overlying sedimentary rocks. The Archean rocks were eroded, or worn away at the top, and submerged deep beneath the sea. They are separated by a profound unconformity, or great time interval, from the overlying sedimentary rocks.

When the seas came in, sediments accumulated upon the smooth surface [of the earlier rocks] to a great depth. These sediments are composed of layers of sandstone, shales, and limestones, and are known as the Grand Canyon Series, or Unkar-Chuar formations, of Algonkian time. Some of the remains of the most primitive life found in the earth's crust are found in these sediments. The fossils reveal the presence of simple plants known as "algae" long before the beginning of the Paleozoic, or "old life" era. When sediments had piled up to a great depth, profound folding took place. This area was lifted high above the surrounding seas. Geologists believe that mountains comparable to the present-day Alps were then present in this vicinity. The slow, disintegrating forces of nature, however, gnawed away at the high mountains until they were finally reduced to lowlying hills and valleys. This area was then submerged beneath the sea. The total thickness of these sediments will never be known, but twelve thousand feet of sediments measuring over two miles in thickness still remain exposed above the Archean rocks. They have been tilted at such angles and worn away to such an extent that at no place do they extend vertically but a few hundred feet at the most. In places, they are entirely missing.

The seas came in over this submerged area and deposited the Tonto Group of Cambrian age. The lowest member of the group, the Tapeats Sandstone, now makes the greater part of the broad Tonto Platform within the Canyon. Above this occurs the Bright Angel Shale and Muav Limestone. These three formations contain the remains of primitive marine forms of extinct life, such as invertebrate tracks, worm trails, shellfish, crustaceans, and seaweed impressions.

The next formation is known as the Redwall Limestone. This deposit of Mississippian age stands out as a true vertical wall some five hundred feet in thickness. . . .

Resting upon the Redwall Limestone occurs a series of cliffs and slopes, making up a total thickness of eight hundred feet. This is the Supai formation [now known as the Supai Group] of Pennsylvanian time. Some of the most primitive reptilian tracks are present in a massive bed near the center of the formation.

Above the Supai formation lie nearly three hundred feet of Hermit Shale of Permian age. This formation is of interest for the abundant occurrence of well-preserved animal tracks, ancient plant impressions, and insect wings. A single wing impression in one instance measured nearly four inches in length.

The next record in the walls of the Canyon is about four hundred feet of Coconino Sandstone of Permian age. This formation is known as the best Permian fossil-track horizon in the world. . . .

The topmost formation in the walls of the Canyon is the Kaibab Limestone of Permian age. A great many species of fossils have been collected from this formation. . . .

Geologists believe that sediments measuring nearly six thousand feet, or over one mile in thickness, once rested on top of the present, topmost layer at the Grand Canyon. The complete succession of these younger formations may be seen in southern Utah, at Bryce Canyon and Zion National Parks.

Later research has revised the age of some formations. For example, the earliest rocks at Grand Canyon are now understood to be younger than Archean. At no more than two billion years old, they fall within the *Proterozoic*, while the term Archean refers to rocks that are considerably older than those found at Grand Canyon.

Further work has also identified several more rock layers in the Canyon. Sometimes these layers were not identified at first because they are thin, or occur only in patches. For example, the Sixtymile Formation, about one hundred twenty feet thick where it occurs in the eastern Canyon, is made up of debris shed into lakes as the Grand Canyon Series uplifted about 830 million years ago. Below the Redwall, the Temple Butte Limestone filled channels cut by streams into the underlying Muav Limestone in the eastern Grand Canyon, but did accumulate to a depth of several hundred feet between the two formations in the western Canyon. The Surprise Canyon Formation later filled just lowlying areas on *top* of the Redwall.

SOME FUCOIDES FROM GRAND CANYON

Edwin D. McKee, Park Naturalist
November, 1932.

IN MANY OF THE SEDIMENTARY FORMATIONS of the Grand Canyon are found peculiar, wormlike ridges of varying shapes and sizes, whose origins have been a matter of considerable speculation. Some of them are known locally as "worms." Geologists call them "fucoides" because of their resemblance in shape to certain seaweeds, especially those of the family *Fucaceae*. As a matter of fact, some of the so-called "fucoides" may have been formed from the impressions of such plants, but many of them very definitely had other origins. . . .

Some of the most interesting but least understood of the fucoides found in Grand Canyon come from the bright red shales of the Dox Formation (Algonkian age). As with most fucoides, they represent the natural casts of depressions occurring on the old mud surfaces. . . . They are found associated with the casts of ripplemarks, the square molds of salt crystals, and the casts of shrinkage cracks in mud.

PAGES IN CAMBRIAN HISTORY

Edwin D. McKee, Park Naturalist
May, 1930.

GEOLOGICAL PICKS IN HAND, we were examining the green shales of the Tonto Platform in the lower part of the Grand Canyon. A fascinating pastime this, for while investigating the flat, slabby layers of that level, we were actually exploring the muds and fine sands which long ages ago were accumulating on an ocean bottom, and over which various primitive forms of life crawled and swam. To the geologists, these rocks represent a period of history known as the Cambrian. The forms of life preserved in these rocks include the oldest definite traces of animals. . . .

It is interesting to note that the ancient and once world-ruling race of trilobites made their debut in seas of Cambrian age, some of whose outlines are now represented by rocks of the Tonto Platform of Grand Canyon. It is further noteworthy that the trilobites made their last appearance among the sands and limes of the Permian Period, some of which were later changed to the rocks now forming the Grand Canyon rim. The dwarfed trilobites which are found there in the Kaibab Limestone may be considered a part of the last stand of the race preceding its total extinction. In brief, the rocks exposed in the walls of the Grand Canyon tell the story of both the rise and the fall of the oldest group of animals to have left distinct records for modern man.

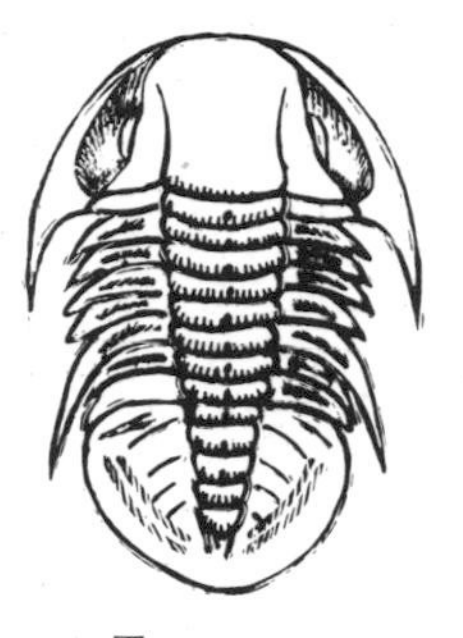
TRILOBITE

CRINOIDAL LIMESTONE

Edwin D. McKee, Park Naturalist
October, 1931.

FIVE OF THE FOURTEEN MAJOR DIVISIONS—or formations—in the walls of the Grand Canyon are largely or entirely composed of limestone. The conditions under which these were formed varied extremely, and in most cases are not yet entirely understood. Limestones may be formed (1) by bacterial precipitation, (2) as the result of photosynthesis of plants, (3) by evaporation . . . (4) by mechanical deposition of calcium carbonate fragments, (5) by a change of conditions allowing the escape of CO_2 from water, and (6) through the accumulation and cementation of organic structures. The Bass Limestone and limey parts of the Chuar and Supai formations are known to have been formed as reefs by the action of primitive plants (algae). Limestone deposited as travertine in recent times is found in many places in Grand Canyon, notably around the waterfalls of Havasu Creek, while many of the other limestones of Grand Canyon were formed from the skeletal remains of sea animals.

One of the finest possible examples of limestone formed from the remains of marine animals was recently discovered in the Redwall formation of Grand Canyon. About midway in that stratum, where the Kaibab Trail passes, is a layer about ten feet in thickness which at first glance appears to be composed of crumbly sand. Closer examination, however, shows that the material is actually a mass of crystals of the mineral calcite, and that these preserve the forms of multitudes of crinoid stems (sea lilies). In most parts of this layer the crinoids make up the entire rock, but in some areas the rather well-preserved shells of another sea animal (*Spirifer centronatus*) are found associated with them. . . .

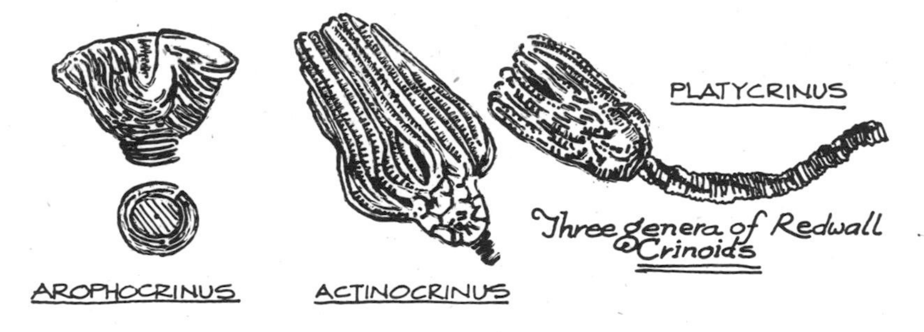

These sea lilies or stone lilies, so-called because of their similarity in appearance to plants with long stems, were marine animals which were abundant in the seas of the past, and are represented by nearly six hundred living species. They are sedentary or stalked forms related to the starfish and sea urchins. They are composed of a crown and a stalk, the latter usually six to eighteen inches in length. The stalks consist of many superimposed, disc-like, perforated pieces called columnals, and these are the parts most commonly found in fossil form. The sea lilies are usually found at moderate depths, although there are a few deep-sea and shallow water types.

They feed on microscopic plants and animals.

In the Jurassic period, the crinoids or sea lilies reached their greatest size—fifty feet high with crowns a yard wide—but long before that, in the early part of the Mississippian period, they had reached the stage of greatest abundance both of species and individuals.

THE FLORA OF THE HERMIT SHALE IN GRAND CANYON

Dr. David White
December, 1929.

THE UPPER PART, including nearly three hundred feet, of the great series of redbeds found in the walls of the Grand Canyon is known as the Hermit Shale. . . . The sediments are freshwater-laid, mainly rather fine, more-or-less distinctly angular sand grains, thinly coated with red oxide of iron. The shales are stream ripple-bedded and wavy. . . .

The lower part, at least, of the formation was laid down by streams, first gradually filling the old drainage system, and later building up a floodplain over the "Esplanade" Sandstone. The streams were more-or-less intermittent, with dry intervals. . . .

Fragments of plants are found, generally rare, in the sandstones in the stream-rippled sandy shale and in the slime layers, which sometimes also show in great distinctness footprints made by several kinds of primitive reptiles and amphibians, while the slimy surfaces freshly exposed by the withdrawal of the water were still moist. . . .

The Hermit plants embrace a number of European conifers and seedbearing plants found in Europe or closely related to European species, but about half of the flora has not been known before.

LAOPORUS GOES WALKING

Edwin D. McKee, Park Naturalist
August, 1929.

THE MYSTERIOUS COCONINO SANDSTONE, which extends as a sheer wall and a mighty white band around the upper reaches of the Grand Canyon . . . has once again disclosed one of its records of ancient history.

. . . [W]hen the sand was soft and unconsolidated some hundreds of millions of years ago, animal life—prehistoric reptiles or amphibians—walked over its surface. Although these creatures have themselves completely disappeared we know not where, their tracks, their footprints, still remain to tell and to show us the undeniable story. . . .

One of the most characteristic and abundant of the ichnite [trace] fauna of this history possesses the striking and distinguished name of *Laoporus noblei*. Laoporus was an animal probably of lizardlike proportions. Dr. Lull, the namer, gave the following description of it: "The creatures which made the footprints were quadrupeds of moderate size with broad, stumpy feet, apparently clawed, and having at least four toes in front and five behind. . . . The limbs were apparently short, with a wide trackway implying a bulky body. No trace of a dragging tail is discernible on any of the specimens, and the body was carried clear of the ground."

A PROBABLE INFLUENCE ON LIFE IN THE KAIBAB SEA

Edwin D. McKee, Park Naturalist
February, 1934.

THROUGHOUT MOST OF THE SIX HUNDRED FOOT thickness of sand and limestone which makes up the Kaibab formation of Grand Canyon, silica occurring chiefly in the form of chert is a very conspicuous feature. Many of the

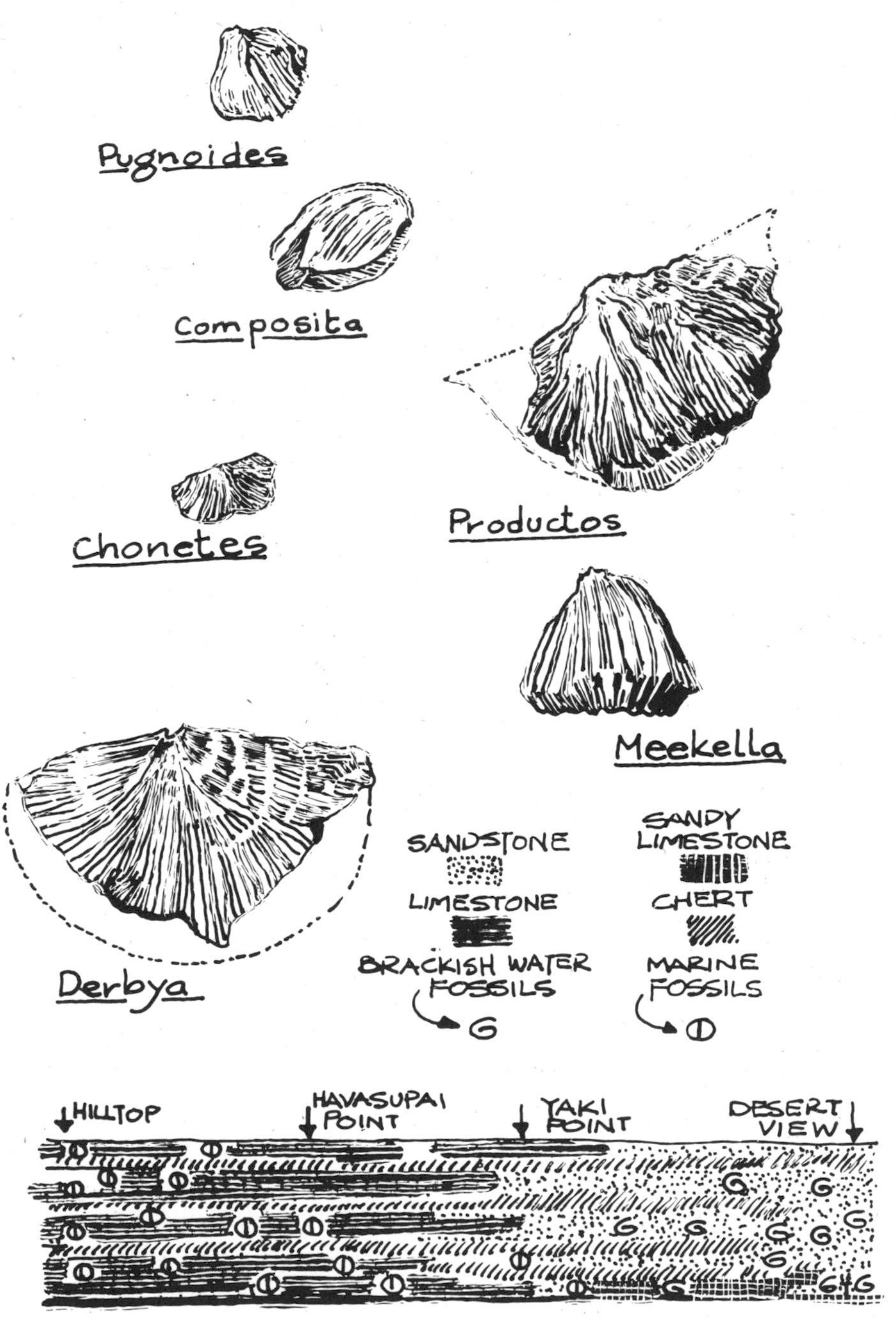

MAIN CLIFF OF KAIBAB FORMATION IN THE GRAND CANYON

locally abundant fossils have shells which are petrified, showing that unquestionably in some cases lime has been replaced by silica as a secondary development. Furthermore, many of the abundant concretions and nodules, some of which are developed about sponges, suggest secondary origin. On the other hand, certain cherts, which occur as bands and which are chalky white except where a brown iron rust has developed on the surface, are almost surely the result of the original deposition of silica. The prominent bands of this hard but brittle material actually form, in the area of Grand Canyon Village, nearly fifty percent of the great massive cliff that constitutes the upper part of the formation. . . .

If we consider as a unit the massive, sandy limestone which forms the largest cliff of the Kaibab formation, we find that the sea whose deposits it represents varied considerably from east to west in the short distance represented in Grand Canyon National Park. Toward the west, the chert bands are at a minimum and fossils of an open sea type are most abundant; toward the east near the Kaibab trail, the reverse is true. . . .

This would make a very favorable condition for streams to gather colloidal silica from the rather pure sands [of the shore], and would account for the marked concentration of the chert beds resulting from its precipitation on the borders of the sea.

OBSERVATION

May, 1934.

A SHARK'S TOOTH was found embedded in limestone of the Kaibab formation below Desert View Point in March. The specimen was referred to Dr. L. Hussakof of the American Museum of Natural History who kindly identified it. He writes: "the specimen is *Deltodus mercurii*, Newberry, 1876."

REMNANTS OF THE AGE OF DINOSAURS ON SOUTH RIM OF GRAND CANYON

Edwin D. McKee, Park Naturalist
August, 1934.

IN 1858, DR. J.S. NEWBERRY, GEOLOGIST on Lt. Ives' exploring expedition, recognized in the valley of the Little Colorado River a series of rocks which was definitely above and of later [younger] age than the highest which he had seen exposed in the walls of Grand Canyon. . . .

Among a large accumulation of data, two things appear to have especial significance. First, since the remnants of these strata are found north, south, east, and west of Grand Canyon, and since they are known to have been formed during the Triassic period (first part of the "Age of Dinosaurs"), it is clearly evident that rocks of this age once covered the entire Grand Canyon area. Second, these remnants furnished evidence that a long period of erosion and wearing away of the region occurred just prior to the beginning of actual Grand Canyon cutting.

THE YOUTHFUL GRAND CANYON

Edwin D. McKee, Park Naturalist
March, 1930.

THE TRANSLATION OF GEOLOGICAL PERIODS to age estimates in terms of years is a process involving many uncertainties. Numerous methods have been employed in making such determinations, though the latest and most generally approved one—that of radioactivity—places the age limits of various geological occurrences considerably farther back in history than did former calculations; by this new method we have today a fairly definite scale of time—approximate to be sure—yet probably fairly accurate, upon which we may base our estimates. The results of this scale place the age of Grand Canyon somewhere between seven and nine million years. . . .

The principal value of this estimate of the Canyon's age is found not in its accuracy as an exact number, but in its use as a comparable figure to show the relation of the Canyon's age to that of other features of the region. We find, for example, that the time when the uppermost stratum in the Canyon walls was formed must have been somewhat over two hundred million years ago, and by the same scale, that the old crystallines of the Inner Gorge—rocks of the earliest era in geological history—date back over a billion years. What, then, is the life of our mighty Grand Canyon? Its depths—the results of a youthful stream and the occurrence of recent times by comparison—merely serve to show us the real, abysmal depths of time, which penetrated inconceivably far back in history and serve perhaps even better to place before us the reality of our own insignificance.

Through subsequent research, geologists discovered that the Grand Canyon is even more youthful than believed in McKee's time. Dating of lava flows along the course of the Colorado River show that the river evolved its present course to begin carving the Canyon into the rising plateau less—probably much less—than 5.5 million years ago.

Red Butte

CHAPTER III
River, Sky, and Seasons

THE FIERCE, RESTLESS COLORADO RUSHES THROUGH
THE PRISON OF ITS OWN MAKING

THE CARRYING POWER OF THE COLORADO RIVER

R.L. Nichols, Ranger Naturalist
August, 1930.

THE U.S. GEOLOGICAL SURVEY HAS STATIONED, at the bottom of the Grand Canyon near the mouth of Bright Angel Creek, engineers whose job is to measure the velocity of the river, its depth, width, silt content, discharge, etc.

Among the many interesting facts which they tell us, none is more startling than that the Colorado River, on the average, carries past any given point approximately one million tons of sand and silt every twenty-four hours. I think everyone who has ever been down to the river will agree that although it is too thin to be classed as a solid, it is much too thick to be used as a beverage. . . .

During the first week of August, 1926, there was a series of very heavy thunderstorms upstream, which caused the swollen river to carry past the gauging station near Bright Angel Creek twenty-six million tons of sand and silt during one period of twenty-four hours. . . . The Colorado is indeed a most powerful transporting agent; a mighty river!

The Colorado's sediment load varies with the seasons. It also varies with cycles in the weather, diminishing, for instance, when summer storms decreased on the Colorado Plateau in the 1940s. But overall, the gauging station at Bright Angel once measured an average of three hundred eighty thousand tons of silt per day, before the floodgates of Glen Canyon Dam closed upstream of Grand Canyon in 1963. Now, a daily average of just forty thousand tons of sediment flows through the Canyon, mostly from two tributaries: the Paria and Little Colorado Rivers.

THE COLORADO RIVER

Ralph A. Redburn, Ranger Naturalist
September, 1931.

ASIDE FROM THE GRAND CANYON ITSELF, the Colorado River is the feature of greatest interest at Grand Canyon National Park. It can be seen from both rims in many places, although for the greater part of its length through the Grand Canyon it is very snugly hidden. . . .

The river was first seen in the bottom of the Grand Canyon by Cardenas in the autumn of 1540. Just when the term "Colorado" was first applied is not known. It undoubtedly was given by a Spaniard, who named the river from the color of its water. Often the river is quite red. . . .

The drainage area furnishes a great catchment basin for

rainwater. The better-known tributaries other than the Green and Upper Colorado which feed the Colorado are the San Juan, Fremont, Little Colorado, Paria, Virgin, and the Gila. Each adds its volume to the mass, and thus we have a great accumulation of water.

Still, man has the conquering instinct, and he tries to use the river for material purposes: navigation, irrigation, and domestic use. He at present is trying to harness the Colorado and use its water and the power therefrom for irrigation and to generate power. The United States Reclamation Service, which has worked wonders with other streams even where there seems to be no chance for achievement, is now beginning the construction of the famous Hoover Dam [Boulder Dam], which is located two canyons below Grand Canyon in what is known as Black Canyon. . . .

Prior to the 1963 completion of Glen Canyon Dam, warm, silty waters flooded seasonally through Grand Canyon, replenishing its beaches and sustaining native fish and flora. Since the dam, surges dictated by electrical power demands have eroded the banks of the river and upset its natural dynamics. In 1992, Congress passed the Grand Canyon Protection Act, which mandates that the flow of water through the dam be modified to protect the natural, cultural, Native American, and recreational resources downstream.

. . . [A]side from the tentative irrigation project to which the river will serve water: "What is the good of the Colorado River?" Its chief merit is not utility, but grandeur.

"THE EXPLORER"

M.R. Tillotson, Park Superintendent
January, 1931.

THERE HAS RECENTLY been much legal argument and court procedure with a view to settling the question as to the navigability of the Colorado River. The determination of this feature was one of the primary reasons for the Colorado River expedition made by the War Department in 1857–

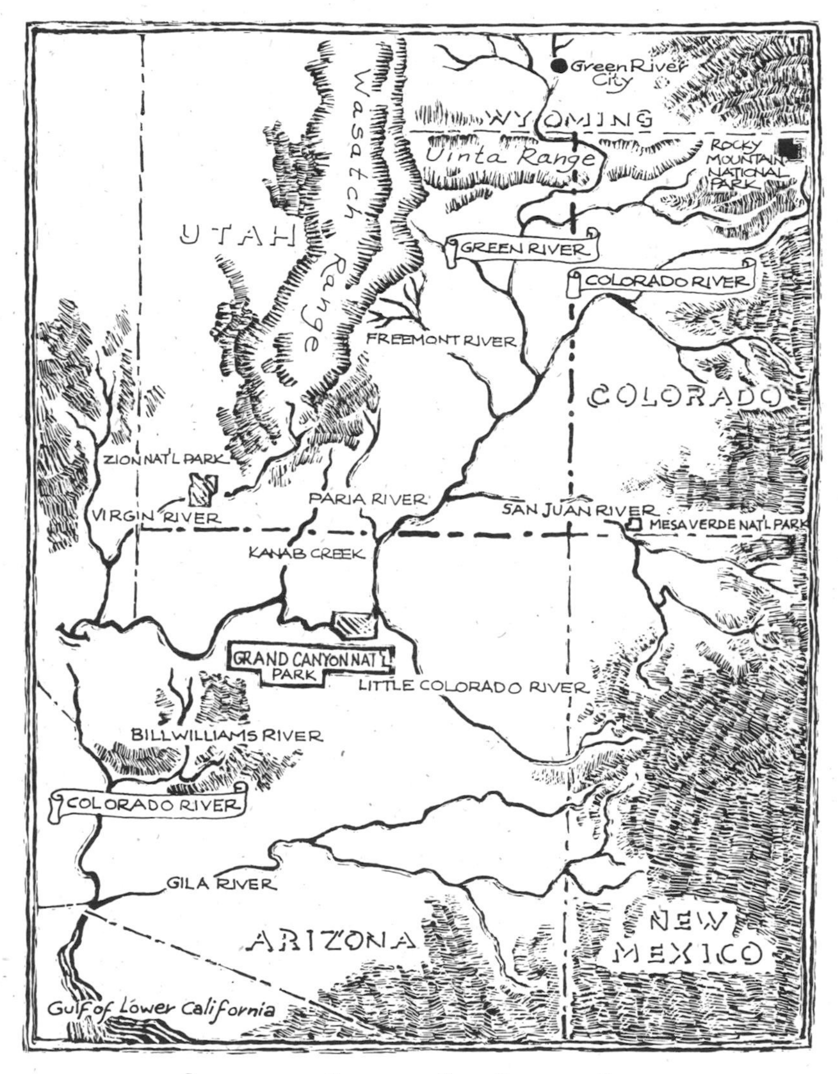

Showing the Colorado River Drainage Basin.

58, under the leadership of Lieutenant Joseph C. Ives of the Corps of Topographical Engineers. . . . Ives soon found that the turbulent Colorado could not be made to serve in this manner as a waterway for the transportation of freight. . . . He states in his official report to the War Department that "the foot of Black Canyon should be considered the practical head of navigation. . . ."

Lieutenant Ives was apparently far more skilled as an explorer and engineer than as a prophet, for we find in his diary a statement made immediately after leaving the only section touched by his expedition which is now in Grand Canyon National Park [the expedition had made their way overland to Havasupai Canyon], to the effect that:

> "Ours has been the first, and will doubtless be the last, party of whites to visit this profitless locality. It seems intended by nature that the Colorado River, along the greater portion of its lonely and majestic way, shall be forever unvisited and undisturbed."

FREDERICK S. DELLENBAUGH 1854–1935

George L. Collins, Assistant Chief Ranger
March, 1935.

A SHORT DISTANCE WEST from Grand Canyon Village and on one of the finest vantage points from which to view the Grand Canyon, there stands a rugged stone memorial honoring those men who accomplished the John Wesley Powell explorations of 1869–1872 along the Colorado River from Green River, Wyoming, to the Virgen River district west of Grand Canyon. . . .

One of the most famous of that group, Frederick Samuel Dellenbaugh, passed away on January 29th of this year, and by his passing closed the final chapter in the earthly histories of its membership. He had been for some years the only remaining survivor.

Mr. Dellenbaugh joined Major Powell at the beginning of what is known as the "second expedition" in the spring of 1871, as artist and topographic assistant to the geologists of the party. Despite his youth, he fully justified the confidence placed in him by his leader in the unrelenting struggle downstream by boat through seventeen tremendous canyons on the then uncharted waters of one of the most treacherous rivers of the world. . . .

Let us remember the thoughts of young Fred Dellenbaugh on issuance, for good and sufficient reasons, of Major Powell's order to terminate the expedition at Kanab Creek. Although worn and fatigued through having along with his fellows put his whole being into the almost superhuman task at hand, he was filled with a lasting regret which he has expressed by saying: "This decision then was, and ever since has been, a matter of great disappointment to me, for I was ready to finish the Grand Canyon."

Major John Wesley Powell's epic voyages down the Colorado River rank among the greatest adventures in American history. A largely self-taught professor of geology at Illinois Wesleyan University, Major Powell set off with a handful of companions in small wooden boats to run the canyons of the Colorado not once, but twice. His detailed, eloquent accounts of these dangerous explorations into a previously unknown region were all the more sensational because Powell had lost his right arm in 1862, at the Civil War battle of Shiloh. Through his research among the native peoples of the West, Powell went on to become the first director of the U.S. Bureau of Ethnology. His knowledge of the topography, hydrology, and geology of the area then led to his appointment as the second director of the U.S. Geological Survey.

WIND RIVERS OF THE GRAND CANYON

George L. Collins, Assistant Chief Ranger
January, 1934.

ALL GRAND CANYON WATERWAYS, including not only the Colorado River but several tributary streams as well, are characterized by their extremely unusual surroundings. They become immediate centers of interest wherever seen because they are practically the only animating features disclosed to view. There is an absorbing interest for anyone in watching the Colorado River's wild rush through its narrow channel deep down within the Grand Canyon. One cannot help but be deeply stirred in such a setting by the strange personality of power, mystery, and loneliness the river manifests. . . .

There are other streams flowing within the Grand Can-

yon—mighty streams, in fact, covering the whole area—they are nevertheless quite ignored by the average visitor simply because he cannot see them. Yet there they are; working more gently and with less concentration than the rivers of water perhaps, but as ceaselessly contributing their share in the general scheme of things. You have guessed by now that the reference is to those other great streams: streams of air which twist and swirl so sleekly in and about the Canyon.

On some cool day you may have witnessed the smoke from Grand Canyon Village flowing along close to the ground and then over the Canyon rim, to tumble down and down into the depths perhaps for some hundreds of feet or more before it disperses.

This sight occurs frequently during periods of cool or cold weather, when smoke hangs heavily and the prevailing wind, in flowing up from the south over gradually elevating land surfaces, becomes steadily colder and heavier until on reaching the rim, a giant air cascade occurs just as would a waterfall. . . .

Grand Canyon Airlines pilots tell us that the prevailing southwest wind averages some 800 feet in depth or thickness. At times it may be much greater, depending, of course, on temperatures and the accompanying fluctuations in density. . . .

As the air stream tumbles down into the Canyon it expands swiftly due to higher temperatures encountered (the difference from rim to bottom being about 15 degrees normally, with a far broader change at times) . . . forming a great updraft or vertical column which, if visible, would certainly appear as a gigantic fountain rising generally over the central portion of the Canyon.

. . . Sometimes there is immense force shown by this fountain of air. Aviators have passed over the Canyon edge at a thousand feet or more above ground, and after entering the zone of upward flowing air, found their planes steadily elevated for hundreds of feet simply through the lifting power of this current. . . .

Not always by any means, but occasionally, rain will fall into the Canyon and be absorbed by the warmer and drier air near the lowest levels to such degree that only a few drops ever reach the bottom. Inner-canyon trail parties have thus actually passed with no discomfort directly under showers of rain which have given higher reaches of the Canyon a good soaking.

THE BLUE HAZE OF GRAND CANYON

Ralph A. Redburn, Ranger Naturalist, with
Professor Henry Russell, Princeton University
August, 1931.

"WHAT IS THAT BLUE HAZE?" asks the tourist of the ranger, as he looks at one of the most conspicuous features seen in the Grand Canyon.

This beautiful blue film is not due to any queer phenomena. It is natural that it should be here; it is present all over the world, although it is not as noticeable in some regions as in others.

To explain this, one must speak primarily of two things: one, our blue atmosphere; and the other, the reason why this haze is so conspicuous or so intensified in the Canyon.

The atmosphere (*atmo* meaning vapor—*sphaira* meaning

sphere) is a film of gaseous elements which forms a continuous envelope around our earth. . . .

The blue color of the atmosphere comes mainly from the air itself, and is due to the scattering of light by the tiny molecules of which the atmospheric gases are composed. . . .

The higher one gets, whether on a mountain, in an airplane, or a balloon, the darker the blue of the sky becomes simply because there is less air above to scatter the light.

The atmosphere naturally extends down into the very bottom of the Grand Canyon, and because of its blue color, blue haze becomes evident between the walls.

The reason this haze is so conspicuous here is due mainly to two features: the walls acting simultaneously as a background and reflecting agent, and the atmosphere being rather pure and free of dust.

Air pollution now blights this beautiful blue haze. Monitoring begun in the 1950s has revealed steadily deteriorating air quality at the Grand Canyon. In winter, sulfates created by sulfur dioxide from the Navajo Generating Station at Page, Arizona, dramatically reduce visibility up to forty days each year. "Scrubbers" will be installed on the Navajo Generating Station by 1999 to reduce this air pollution. In summer, refineries, industrial and utility sources, and automobile exhaust from southern California often dim Grand Canyon's bright air for several days at a time. Steps are underway to reduce auto and other emissions in California and Arizona cities for health reasons.

GRAND CANYON ILLUMINATED BY AURORA BOREALIS

M.R. Tillotson, Park Superintendent
July, 1928.

ONE OF THE MOST BEAUTIFUL AND STRIKING of Nature's phenomena, the Aurora Borealis or Northern Lights, was plainly visible from the South Rim of the Canyon Saturday night, July 7th. This appeared as great streamers of light across the entire northern horizon, as if a battery of powerful searchlights in the far distance were being played to illuminate the sky. These streamers were constantly changing in position and intensity, while during the entire evening the horizon in the due north had the appearance of an early gray dawn across the desert. . . .

No satisfactory scientific explanation for the Aurora Borealis has ever been offered, although it is supposed to be due to an electrical disturbance and it is frequently accompanied by interruption of telephone, telegraph, and radio service, and mariners sometimes report an erratic behavior of the compass during the period of these displays.

The appearance of the Northern Lights in these low altitudes is quite unusual, although not altogether previously unknown.

A LUNAR RAINBOW

Paul Kraus, Ranger Naturalist
September, 1933.

ON THE NIGHT OF JULY 7, 1933, between 9:50 and 9:53 o'clock, the eastern arch of a rainbow was seen by the light of a full moon directly to the north of the Utah Parks Lodge [now Grand Canyon Lodge], on the North Rim of the Grand Canyon. The bright moonlight followed a light shower, and the sky was patchy with slowly drifting cumulus clouds. The coloring of the rainbow was so distinct that the series—red, orange, yellow, green, and violet—could be distinguished clearly while the arch slowly faded from the crest downward.

A SIEGE OF FAIR WEATHER

Donald E. McHenry, Junior Park Naturalist
December, 1934.

NOTHING PLEASES THE TOURIST SO MUCH as fair weather for a Canyon visit. Some, however, prefer to see the Canyon when the depths are filled with drifting shadows of numerous small clouds floating above, or perhaps enhanced by an errant storm moving majestically from rim to rim.

It is, however, no aesthetic consideration which leads Grand Canyon inhabitants to long most ardently for more clouds and much more moisture. The annual rainfall for the past thirty years on the North Rim is 26 inches, and 17.3 inches on the South Rim. However, during the year from November 1, 1933, to October 30, 1934, the rainfall for the North Rim has been but 13.4 inches, and only 9.28 inches for the South Rim. Although a delight to visitors, this siege of fair weather for last year has not passed without leaving its mark upon life in Grand Canyon. . . .

Not only the plants, but the animals of the region felt the drought. It was too dry for the usual crop of mushrooms upon which the deer feed with so much relish. Many old reliable waterholes on the North Rim dried up for the first time in their known history. . . .

. . . [W]e at Grand Canyon, along with our friends the Hopi Indians near the Painted Desert to the east, would be pleased to have a few more clouds and considerably more rain than we have had for the past year, the tourist to the contrary notwithstanding.

—Summer—

METEOROLOGICAL DATA

Paul Kraus, Ranger Naturalist
July, 1929.

SNOW AT GRAND CANYON ON JUNE 6 is something worth noting. On that date, the ground on both North and South Rims was white for a short while. Although snowstorms are not uncommon here in May, there are very few records of their occurrence in June.

YAVAPAI CATCHES A BOLT

Earl W. Count, Ranger Naturalist
July, 1929.

JUPITER RECENTLY AFFORDED ME an impromptu chance to write a nature note. One of our frequent thunderstorms was upon us the other day at Yavapai Station, and a crowd of some forty tourists were collected inside waiting for an opportunity to leave. . . . I took hold of the heavy door by its latch, and had almost closed it when there came through that latch a tremendous flash and a bang like that of a huge rifle. Later, a tourist said he thought I had accidentally discharged a revolver from my left hand. The bolt lifted my left leg off the concrete floor. . . . Then the bolt passed, but not before gouging three holes in the floor, each about six inches in diameter and a couple inches deep.

STATIC ELECTRICITY

Harold H. Hawkins, Ranger Naturalist
January, 1935.

ABOUT FOUR O'CLOCK IN THE AFTERNOON of August 3rd, the writer was standing at Precipice Viewpoint on the North Rim with about thirty-five visitors, and pointing to certain features on the Painted Desert. His right hand was grasping an iron railing, and his left arm was extended in the direction of interest over the Canyon. Without warning, there was heard at the ends of his fingers a sound resembling that of a swarm of bees. Quite surprised, he pulled his hand in, and examined the ends of his fingers to ascertain the cause. Of course, seeing nothing wrong he again extended his arm and resumed speaking. Again the same sound was heard, and once more he lowered his arm. At the same time, he called attention of the visitors to the phenomenon. Naturally, they all thrust their arms out over the railing, and the writer noticed a marked decrease in the amount of buzzing at the end of his own hand. . . .

The secret of this interesting experiment was that the extended arms were conducting electricity to the ground through the bodies of the individuals from a cloud, either overhead or nearby, which was heavily charged with static electricity. The seriousness of this experiment, unbeknown to anyone in the group at the time, was that had this cloud been sufficiently charged so that the potential had been great enough, it could have easily attracted a bolt of lightning from any one of the several rainstorms nearby. . . .

THE PATH OF A THUNDERSTORM

Stephen B. Jones, Ranger Naturalist
July, 1929.

SUNDAY, JUNE 30, A THUNDERSTORM passed over the Kaibab Plateau. The lightning was seen from Grand Canyon Lodge to strike a spur of Buddha Temple. We expected a soaking, but the storm passed off to the northwest. Within a few hours, smoke was seen in this direction, and next day the path of the storm could be traced by a line of four fires.

—Fall—

OBSERVATIONS

September, 1921.

THE MULE DEER ON BOTH SIDES of the Canyon began to lose their coats of tan and take on the winter grey about the end of August.

October, 1932.

THE DRY CLASH OF ANTLERS attracted my attention in the early morning of September 18th. Two handsome mule deer bucks were engaged in combat not over seventy-five feet from the North Rim Ranger Station. The contest soon ended with no serious consequences. It gave evidence, however, that mating season had begun in deerdom.

November, 1926.

IT APPEARS THAT about September 28 the tarantulas began their annual parade across the highways on the South Rim of the Canyon. Thirty-four were counted on the east drive between the junctions of the roads leading to Yavapai Point and to Yaki Point. All seemed headed northward.

AUTUMN

November, 1926.

THE DECIDUOUS TREES AND SHRUBS are taking on their autumnal garb of scarlet and golden-brown. The animals are preparing for the more rigorous weather ahead. Skunks totter around on their small feet because of the thick layer of fat they carry around at this season. The beautiful Abert squirrels put in tireless days sending pine nuts to the ground and running to their caches with pine cones. The provident painted chipmunk is busy laying in sufficient supplies to last him throughout the winter. Beaver that have been leading a nomadic life since the high waters in the spring washed out their dams, are back in Bright Angel and Phantom Canyons rebuilding their dams and cutting down their winter wood supply. Deer are appearing in their winter coats and polished horns in anticipation of the courting season. These animals are leaving their summer range at the higher elevations and going to a lower altitude for winter.

—Winter—

WHEN WINTER COMES

Edwin D. McKee, Park Naturalist
January, 1932.

EARLY THIS FALL, THE SUPAI INDIANS were very busy gathering pinyon nuts. They said there was a long, cold winter ahead. When I asked one how he knew, I was told that the abundance of the nut crop gave certain evidence. . . .

Snow has fallen on sixteen different days already this winter (November and December), and on December 12th it covered the ground on the South Rim of Grand Canyon to an average depth of eighteen inches. . . .

The early winter temperatures recorded on the South Rim of the Grand Canyon this year further substantiate the truth of the Supai forecast. On December 13th, the temperature (–5 degrees) was thirteen degrees lower than at any time last year. Unofficial readings made on the Canyon rim the same day even went as low as –18 degrees. . . . Yes, winter has come this year.

FIELD OBSERVATIONS

February, 1932.

DURING THE STORM OF JANUARY 19 TO 21, snow covered the ground and remained even in the bottom of Grand Canyon. It was estimated that between two and three inches of snow fell in the vicinity of Phantom Ranch—an event heretofore unheard of, at least within recent years.

March, 1933.

CHART SHOWING MINIMUM TEMPERATURES DURING PAST FIVE YEARS SOUTH RIM OF GRAND CANYON

	1928–9	1929–30	1930–1	1931–2	1932–3
Nov.	13	16	9	4	24
Dec.	1	17	8	–5	1
Jan.	–1	–5	8	0	1
Feb.	–7	12	18	6	–14
Mar.	8	16	15	5	

AN UNSEASONABLE SEASON

Donald E. McHenry, Junior Naturalist
March, 1934.

THE FOLLOWING TABLE gives comparative meteorological data for the last three winters on the South Rim, including a period from November 11th to February 20th in each case. . . .

	1931–2	*1932–3*	*1933–4*
Total snowfall	87.9″	67.4″	10.5″
Greatest single snowfall	11.5″	8.0″	4.0″
Average monthly mean temperature	27.5	32.3	37.8
Average monthly mean Max. temperature	41.2	45.8	49.7
Average monthly mean Min. temperature	19.4	18.9	26.0

—Spring—

OBSERVATIONS

April, 1930.

THE MOURNING CLOAKS (*Vanessa antiopa*) coming out of hibernation were the first butterflies to make their appearance this spring. On March 14th—an early, warm day—quite a number of these made their appearance around Indian Gardens in the Canyon.

MARCH 23RD APPEARS TO HAVE BEEN the first day of spring at Grand Canyon this year. On that date, chestnut-back bluebirds, chipping sparrows, a song sparrow, and some gray-crowned rosy finches were all seen for the first time this season.

May, 1934.

THE WHITE-THROATED SWIFT WAS SEEN DARTING about Grandview Point in Grand Canyon on March 25 this year. This is a full week ahead of the earliest previous date on record of the arrival of this species: April 4, 1932.

SPRING IS NEAR

Donald E. McHenry, Junior Naturalist
March, 1932.

SPRING IS NEAR—at least as close as three thousand feet below the South Rim. . . . The writer stepped off the South Rim on March 10th in about a foot of snow, and continued to wade and slip through winter during the first drop of about one thousand feet into the Canyon. . . .

Here, the tender green of the new young leaves of the narrowleaf mountain mahogany and its cousin, the broadleaf mountain mahogany, shone brilliantly against the weather-beaten green of the somber juniper and the glossy hollygrape. Here and there, snuggled close to the ground, were groups of youthful leaves giving promise of lovely evening primroses in the not too distant future. A little farther down the trail, just at the foot of the Redwall cliffs, a few clumps of rabbitbrush showed dabs of green where spring was beckoning the new leaves from the gaunt and winter-worn twigs. . . .

MOURNING CLOAK

This brought the writer to the vicinity of the Indian Gardens. A shower of the queer little catkins of the cottonwoods fell all about as he walked through the thickets of new pussywillows which all but completely hedged in Garden Creek. . . . Here and there on the way towards the drop into the Inner Gorge, the Apache plume had spread its leaves to welcome springtime.

Weaving back and forth beneath the sinister cliffs which guarded the mouth of Pipe Creek, one met spring on every hand. An observant person would catch the flitting of that dark-winged butterfly—the mourning cloak—as she darted through the green foliage of arrowweed. Some of the early leaves of the cranesbill spread their palmlike foliage to the sun from the rocky slopes along the trail.

Indeed, spring is very near when one can stand on the Canyon rim and see the gray of the winter vegetation along the upper watercourses shade into the delicate green of spring below. Perhaps it will come climbing up the Canyon walls very soon. When it does, it will lend even more color to our already resplendent Canyon, and warm the hearts of those who will welcome the passage of winter.

LIFE SCIENCE

CHAPTER IV
Life Zones, Plant Succession, and Flora

. . . ENVIRONMENT

Chester R. Markley, Park Ranger
January, 1931.

HERE WE STAND, ON THE BRINK of that magnificent gorge which the mighty forces of nature have cut from solid rock. Across that fearful span of spectacular splendor, we see the spruce, fir, and aspen forest type characteristic of Canada: the Canadian Life Zone. Dropping our glance just the slightest to the very rim itself, we see the yellow pine forest type of Colorado: the Transition Life Zone. Lowering the head just a trifle until our glance passes right beneath the North Rim, we see the pinyon-juniper forest type, typical of the arid West. This is the Upper Sonoran Life Zone. And then, as we look lower and lower down in the shadowy depths of the Canyon, we see the end of the treeline, where the desert shrubs and cacti of Mexico meet our eyes: the Lower Sonoran Life Zone.

IRREGULARITIES IN CLIMATIC-BELTS

Clyde C. Searl, Ranger Naturalist
September, 1929.

IN NO PLACE IS ECOLOGY—the science which deals with the relationships of plants and animals to their environments—better explained than in the life zones of Grand Canyon. In few places can a greater number of climatic belts be found in such a small area, and for this reason the ecologist finds himself in a paradise. . . .

In a place built of sheer walls and plateaus such as in Grand Canyon and the surrounding country, the ecologist finds many irregularities in the climatic belts. . . .

Exposure is directly affected by steepness of slope. This is plainly seen in all areas at the base of cliffs. The cliffs either allow the maximum amount of sunlight, or they hide and shade the areas beneath. The west [-facing] and south [-facing] slopes of the Canyon receive a great amount of direct heat from the sun, and forest and plant formations will run higher on such slopes. The cooler areas are the north [-facing] and east [-facing] slopes because of their protection from the rays of the sun; beneath these, forest and plant groups will naturally grow much lower than the average boundary of their life zones in the region. . . .

Insolation naturally follows exposure. Normal temperatures fall with increase in altitude, about one degree fahrenheit for each rise of three hundred thirty feet. Such being the case, one should expect a decrease of at least eighteen degrees in temperature going from Phantom Ranch to Grand Canyon Lodge on the North Rim. However, the range in temperature is usually greater, due to the deep and narrow features of the Canyon and the characteristic of the rock masses to hold heat.

A LIVING CONQUEST

Earl W. Count, Ranger Naturalist
July, 1930.

HEAR THEN THE STORY OF A LIVING CONQUEST, where from humble beginnings and at uncounted cost, living nature has contrived to turn even this hot and dry region into a place where it is good to dwell.

The wanderer along the rim sees the orange-colored lichens and their black, dead remains clinging to the bare rock surfaces. These lichens are life's vanguard . . . seeds of a higher order of plant life reach their debris by chance; and from those, there slowly emerge such flower-bearing plants as are willing to lead a hard life. . . . But as the end of winter and the middle of summer bring these plants two separate seasons for gathering their water, some of them bloom and make seeds twice a year. They grow, and their roots take advantage of more cracks in the rock, and crowd the rock to pieces. They die, and their remains give more soil for other and greater but less pioneering hosts to move in and take up the struggle. At last the pine trees tramp in, and in the ungrateful way of living things, they overshadow those who made their living possible. . . .

But again life is artless, and on the pines and junipers come the seeds of the mistletoes. They reach their degenerate little roots down into the juicy branches of the trees to draw their water supply, and grow their berries that the birds will swallow, but the seeds thereby discharge into new territory yet again. . . .

Nature, you will observe, is inconsistent; how much more rapid the conquest if there were no dissension in the invading ranks! But perhaps—may there not be in Nature a deeper philosophy, a more subtle kind of cooperation than limited and therefore necessarily "efficient" man at first surmises?

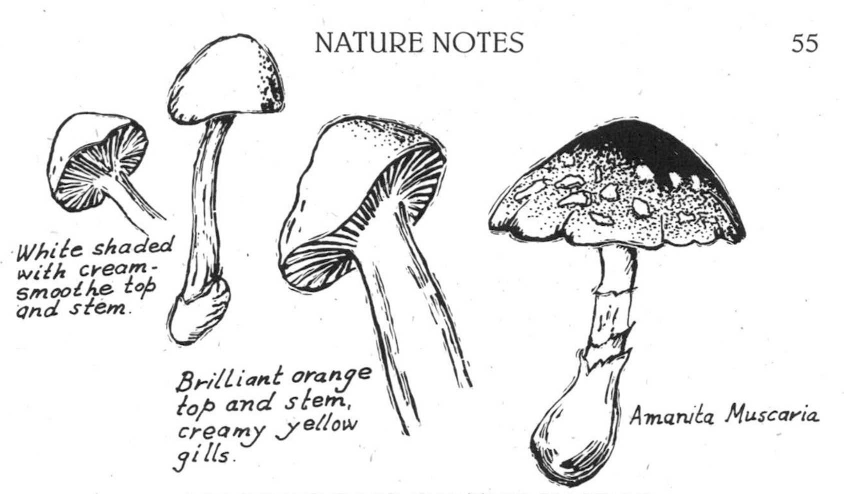

MUSHROOMS ON THE KAIBAB

Laura E. Mills
September, 1929.

ABUNDANT SUMMER RAINS MEAN MUSHROOMS in some places, and the Kaibab is one of those places. . . .

Among the most abundant are the *Boletus*, which have tubes or pores on the undersurface instead of gills. Of these we found three species: the orange-cap, which the deer liked far better than we did; the brown-topped one, for which neither we nor the deer cared at all; and the pale, tan, sticky-topped one, the most plentiful of the three, which was a prime favorite of both the deer and us. . . .

A curious mushroom is the star puffball, dried specimens of which we found before the rains began. Like the other puffballs, it scatters its spores in a little cloud of "smoke" when stepped on, or when any sudden pressure is applied to its "ball." . . .

The deer did not seem to be troubled by any questions as to whether any particular species of mushroom was edible or not; although they did not appear to care for some kinds which we had tried and proved harmless, they devoured some kinds which we were sure were poisonous . . . we put out one of the brilliant vermilion *Amanita muscaria*, and the big buck that roams the North Rim campground gobbled it up as if he were afraid someone might take it away from him, and he seemed none the worse for it, either then or the next day.

Just what part of the diet of the Kaibab squirrel consists of mushrooms would be difficult to say, but we found many of the fungi bearing the marks of squirrel and chipmunk tooth, and saw one squirrel run off through the yellow pines carrying a white mushroom about the size of a hen's egg.

THE GEASTER, OR EARTH STAR

Professor H.V. Hibbard
August, 1928.

QUITE NATURALLY, THE LIFE PURPOSE of this fungus, for fungus it is and of the puffball variety, is to scatter its spores and so, Caliban-like, seed the earth with its own progeny. In this worthy attempt it does not wait to catch onto moving things for a free ride, but hitches along over the ground on its own skinny legs, puffing out its cloudy spores at every jolt and leaving an erratic track in the dust or sand.

Hygroscopy, not muscularity, is the secret of its automotive power. Hygroscopy by interpretation means only a highly sensitive response to slight changes in moisture; and so the starry rays of geaster more or less wiggle abroad over the surface of the ground. . . .

EARTH STAR

Earth star first appears above the ground as a little, soft, white ball about the size of a marble, then when it is ripe . . . it breaks away, peels back the skin in the five or six star-rayed segments which curve back under and support the ball, and away it starts on the fruition of its life purpose.

BROOMRAPE, A ROOT PARASITE

Pauline Mead Patraw
May, 1931.

BETWEEN YAKI AND GRANDVIEW POINTS near the Canyon rim, I found a little yellowish-purple, leafless plant growing near a group of sagebrush. It was in bloom; the flower was a dull yellow color with purple veins and the petal lobes were purple tipped. At first sight I thought recklessly: "a member of the Indian Pipe family!" But upon closer examination, I saw that the tubular flower was irregular, two-lipped, more like that of a figwort.

After considerable digging, I found that this plant was parasitic on the roots of sagebrush. It was attached to the end of the main root. In some cases, this root was swollen where it had been attacked, and there was an excess growth of small laterals. . . .

This is the first record of broomrape at the Grand Canyon, and the only member of this family (*Orobanchaceae*) found here thus far. . . .

Broomrape, judging from the number and position of the specimens found, is probably parasitic on roots of other plants as well as sagebrush. In those cases observed, this parasitism did not appear to have any injurious effect on the host.

MARIPOSA LILY

Laura E. Mills
August, 1929.

ALONG THE ROADSIDE AMONG THE SAGEBRUSH, or scattered under the yellow pines, nods the dainty white mariposa lily (*Calochortus nutalli*), variously called mariposa lily, butterfly tulip, and sego lily. In the drier sections where it springs up under the sheltering sagebrush, its slender stems and very narrow leaves pass unnoticed until crowned by the flower with its brownish-purple markings inside the bases of the petals. . . .

One wonders how such a fragile-appearing member of the lily family can survive the dry seasons and the ravages of animals. Several inches deep in the soil, the plant stores its energy in a solid little starchy bulb. In many places in the West, this bulb was sought by the Indians as a desirable food. It is a favorite food of rodents, and the tops are eaten by deer and cattle.

Nod on, little *Calochortus*! We like you best by the roadside, or under the whispering pines.

PRINCE'S PLUME: A NEW MUSTARD RECORD

Donald E. McHenry, Junior Naturalist
May, 1932.

MANY PEOPLE WHO VISIT THE GRAND CANYON in spring are greatly surprised when they learn that the slopes far below them are not the barren rocks which they seem, but are in reality magnificent wildflower gardens. Indeed, here can be seen such a medley of color as would well make people of a more moist climate envious. Here the azure blue of the penstemon and the desert mint vie for supremacy with the various shades of reds, pinks, and salmons of the paintbrush, the sand verbena, the desert mallow, the cactus, and the wild four o'clock. The cream-colored cliffrose, exhausting the spring air with its heavy incense, looks down on the delicate lavender of the swaying mariposa lily, while here and there beneath the ivory white of the nodding yucca blossom is scattered the brilliant yellow of the paperflower and the golden aster. Everywhere are found many of the lesser members of the flowering sisterhood.

Not least of all this riotous display is the bright yellow of the prince's plume. And what name could be more appropriate for these spikes of fluffy golden flowers? They form an imposing display as they rise from their green clumps of straggly leaves, growing along a sandy, sun-baked slope. Few would guess that there is a first cousin of the lowly cabbage, or that these two plants belong to the mustard family.

Some botanists call the mustards *Cruciferae*, from the fact that the flowers have four petals arranged in the form of a cross.

WEEDS

Clyde C. Searl, Ranger Naturalist
July, 1932.

THE DEFINITION of the word "weed" is necessarily very broad, and its application determined by the uses, either good or noxious, of a plant. Many plants which are harmful to some people are a great boon to others. Weeds are often introduced, either accidentally or purposely, from foreign countries.

In the Grand Canyon National Park, as throughout the entire West, are a number of plants introduced from other countries. Some have been in the region so long and are so common and widespread that it is often a surprise to people to learn that they are not native. Some such plants at Grand Canyon are the

PRINCE'S PLUME

white pigweed or lambs quarters, the common horehound, malva or cheeseweed, and filaree, all having been introduced from Europe.

Two of the most recent arrivals in the Grand Canyon National Park are the Russian thistle and the common mullein. To refer to the Russian thistle as a noxious weed would not hold good in all localities. In many places of the middle west, it is cut when young and used as a forage for stock. It was probably introduced into the Grand Canyon region by means of baled hay brought in to feed mules and horses used by the Government and Fred Harvey interests. At the present time, the growth of this plant is thick through the open spots near the village and along the trails leading into the canyon, where it matures and becomes a tumbleweed. . . .

The common mullein, naturalized from Europe and common in the pine belt of the western part of the United States, is very rapidly getting a foothold in Grand Canyon National Park in spite of protective measures. During 1931, a program of hoeing was carried on along the road leading to Desert View, but this season the growth is heavier than ever.

Among the exotic plants most conspicuous today are the tamarisk trees that now line the banks of the Colorado River. Tamarisk was introduced in the 1930s from the Middle East, in the hope of stabilizing the Colorado's riverbanks. It has done just that, but it is no longer considered beneficial. This delicate-looking tree with its clouds of tiny pink flowers has proved to be a tough, greedy invader; it spreads quickly up watercourses, consuming the available water and crowding out native plants and trees. Tamarisk is so firmly established over so wide an area that it is unlikely any method will be found to eradicate it.

CANYON RIM ROSES

Glen E. Sturdevant, Park Naturalist
August, 1927.

IN SPITE OF THE OLD ADAGE, "ROSES ARE RED,—," in this case they are yellow and white. Perhaps the most conspicuous, as well as the most fragrant, is the cliffrose

(*Cowania mexicana*) [now *Purshia stansburiana*]. This shrub—the tallest of the five roses [at Grand Canyon]—resembles a young cedar in bloom rather than a rose. . . . The exceedingly fragrant, pale yellow flowers, followed by the long, plumelike attachment to the seed, never fail to attract attention. . . .

Another rose closely resembling the former is the Apache plume (*Fallugia paradoxa*). This rose reaches a height of about four feet. The smaller size and the more scattered arrangement of the white flowers make the Apache plume inconspicuous beside the cliffrose. Like the cliffrose, to each seed is attached a plumelike tail as an assurance of wide distribution by the wind.

The fernbush (*Chamaebatiaria millefolium*) is covered with clusters of small white flowers not unlike strawberry blossoms. The numerous, fernlike leaves and bushy appearance of this three-foot shrub quite conceal the cherrylike stems.

Perhaps the most interesting, as well as the smallest of the five roses in bloom, is the lime-loving rock rose (*Petrophytum caespitosum*). This one resembles a moss until the flowers appear in August. Growing as it does with very little moisture and without appreciable soil, this fragrant rose is found occupying small patches and spreading over the bare limestone like so many mats of moss. The rock rose is a prolific bloomer.

SEEDS OF SOME GRAND CANYON WILDFLOWERS

Pauline Mead, Ranger Naturalist
August, 1930.

DURING THE SPRING AND SUMMER, wildflowers bloom in abundance under the pinyons and junipers of the Grand Canyon region. First the sego lilies and delphiniums, later the many varieties of brightly colored penstemons, lupines, and wild geraniums, and finally in the fall, the purple asters appear. Some, such as the cliffrose, bloom throughout the three seasons.

In October and November, the woods begin to look desolate, and a few of the last bright oak and serviceberry leaves cover the ground as though to compensate for the loss of the flowers.

Poking about among the leaves one day in late October in search of geranium seeds for a wildflower garden, my attention was directed toward a group of cup-like pods arranged in a ring around the elongated style of a withered flower. . . . As the seeds had become ripe and the flower parts dry, the pod had pulled away from its pocket at the base of the style, at the same time splitting halfway open, and then by a sudden curling up of the style fiber to which it was still attached, the seed had been thrown from the pod some little distance away. . . . It is by this ingenious mechanism that the wild geranium scatters its unwinged seeds.

Wild Geranium Seed Pods

There are many things concerning the wildflowers that are interesting to watch even after the colored petals have fallen. Winged seeds of several members of the rose family help to beautify the woodland in the autumn. . . .

The wild buckwheat, or sulphurflower, uses the petals of the dead flower as wings. . . .

The small black seeds of the thistle poppy, which are covered with regular rows of tiny bumps, fill the open pockets of the pod. The four ribs of the pod stay in place while the softer divisions between the ribs curl back, releasing the seeds. . . .

In the case of the mallow, each seed has a papery case of its own. These cases are arranged in a circle, forming a green ball to begin with. When the pods dry, they open at the top and separate, spreading out like the petals of a flower, the seeds dropping to the ground.

SAGEBRUSH IN GRAND CANYON NATIONAL PARK

Donald E. McHenry, Junior Naturalist
April, 1932.

HAVE YOU EVER SEEN THE BUSH which makes patches of open country along the Canyon rim appear covered with a gray-green haze? Or perhaps you have seen it stretching as far as the eye could see across some western prairie? Then you have seen the sagebrush. Here and there, this shrub will be found mixing its dusty green with the flaming scarlet of the penstemon and the brilliant yellow of the wild buckwheat. What a riotous bouquet then greets the traveler! Nor can one readily forget the intoxicating perfume which saturates the lazy spring air after a warm shower has kissed sage-land. . . .

One will find at least nine relatives of our sagebrush in the Grand Canyon National Park. None are as conspicuous as is the sagebrush itself, but most give the same pungent odor, especially when the leaf is crushed between the fingers. In fact this odor, together with the gray-green sage color, is a handy way by which most members of the family can be recognized in the field.

Some visitors to the Canyon confuse the sagebrush with the bushes which cover the Tonto Platform. If one examines these plants closely, he may be surprised to learn that they are members of the rose family, called *Coleogyne ramosissima*, or burrobush.

THE YUCCA: SWORDLIKE YET FRIENDLY

Barbara Hastings McKee
January, 1932.

WHILE THERE ARE SEVERAL SPECIES OF YUCCA, the one of greatest economic interest to the original inhabitants of this part of the country is the *Yucca baccata*, or wideleaf yucca. This plant lives in both Upper and Lower Sonoran Zones and seems to thrive in rocky, dry soil. Normally it blooms every year, sending up a flower stalk from the center of the bunch of spear-like leaves. The flowers, of which there are a great many on the stalk, are bell-shaped and creamy white. Later, green fruit hangs from the stalk and ripens with a peach-pink color. It is heavy and solid, having somewhat the shape of a fat, stubby banana. When the fruit dries, it turns brown and becomes very light in weight. The seeds fall to the ground and are scattered; each one of which may be a potential plant.

Hopi Man with Basket Made of Split Yucca Leaves

A FOOD PLANT OF THE INDIANS

Barbara Hastings, Ranger Naturalist
July, 1929.

ONE OF THE MOST STRIKING PLANTS in both Upper and Lower Sonoran Zones in the Grand Canyon is the mescal (*Agave utahensis*), one of the many species of century plants. Starting with a few spiked leaves, it grows probably thirty or forty years into a mature plant, large and well armed with long, bayonetlike, jagged, sawtoothed leaves radiating from the compact center. During the many years of its growth, it stores up food in this center in preparation for the day when it shall send up its flowerstalk. Finally, one spring when enough has been stored up, a huge flowerstalk shoots up from the center and grows rapidly to a height of ten to eighteen feet. The upper two-thirds of the straight stalk bears a large number of beautiful yellow, lilylike, nectar-bearing flowers, each of which later develops a many-seeded capsule. After this supreme effort the agave dies, its duty fulfilled and thousands of new plants started on their long life cycle.

OBSERVATION

H.A. Montgomery, Park Engineer
June, 1934.

ON MARCH 26 & 27, 1934, I obtained some accurate measurements of the growth of [the flowerstalk of] a century plant (*Agave utahensis*), on the Tonto Platform along the Clear Creek Trail about four miles from Phantom Ranch, the results of which are given herewith:

March 26th	9:00 a.m.	32-7/8 inches above the ground.
March 26th	3:30 p.m.	37-1/4 inches above the ground.
March 27th	8:00 a.m.	43 inches above the ground.
March 27th	4:00 p.m.	49-1/4 inches above the ground.

OUR CACTUSES

Pauline Mead, Ranger Naturalist
April, 1930.

CACTUS ARE NATIVE to the Americas only. . . . The structure of the cactus is highly specialized, to meet the conditions imposed upon it by the severe hot and dry climate in which it lives. . . .

The plant can store enough water to keep it alive during long periods of drought—six or ten years—and evaporation of water from the surface is greatly reduced due to a thick, cutinized surface. The water storage cells contain much mucilage of water-holding power. The presence of certain starches is related to water imbibition, and consequently to the swelling and growth of the cactus. Particles of starch exhibit a greater imbibing power in the presence of acid, so that the greater the concentration of acid in the plant, the greater will be its water imbibing capacity.

WHERE OUR CACTI GROW

Pauline Mead Patraw
June, 1931.

IT IS WHILE THE CACTUS IS IN FLOWER that one is best able to find the otherwise dull and inconspicuous plants, and more readily to observe where they grow, and what type of soil and what degree of sunlight and shade they prefer. When transplanting cacti to our wildflower gardens, I learned to look for the hedgehog cactus on the pinyon forest floor where there is considerable shade, but to go to the exposed rocky regions for the pincushion cactus. The prickly pear was always easy to find, since it apparently grew equally well in the forest, on the rocky uplands, and in the small, dry, canyon bottoms. . . .

Prickly Pear Cactus

BOTANICAL NOTE

Edwin D. McKee, Park Naturalist
August, 1931.

PRICKLY PEAR CACTUS, *Opuntia sp.*, recently collected near Coconino Wash, demonstrated fully the adaptation of the root system of this species to the arid climate. Although the plant above the roots was comparatively small (five and one half inches high), and was composed of only two main and five secondary joints, its root system extended for the remarkable distance of five feet eleven inches.

CATSCLAW (ACACIA GREGGII)

Glen E. Sturdevant, Park Naturalist
December, 1926.

THE CATSCLAW FOUND GROWING within the Grand Canyon is one of the few acacias indigenous to the United States.

The catsclaw is a much-branched shrub attaining a height of ten to fifteen feet, with a diameter of four to six inches. The leaves along the young twigs are arranged in a pinnate, or featherlike manner. The flat, brown seeds are nearly circular. Leaves, and a few of the seedpods, still remain upon the shrub at this season of the year.

This shrub thrives in a desertlike region, such as is found within the Grand Canyon. Within the park, it is distributed along the washes above the Tonto Plateau [sometimes called in these pages the Tonto Platform], where it affords but a scanty covering to the soil. These washes are usually dry, but the growth of acacia along them suggests the presence of water within a short distance beneath the surface. The common name is fittingly appended to this small tree or shrub because of the hooked spines along the twigs.

PINYON PINE (PINUS EDULIS)

Glen E. Sturdevant, Park Naturalist
May, 1926.

THIS TREE IS A SMALL, STUNTED PINE rarely exceeding fifty feet in height and two and one-half feet in diameter. When fully mature, it averages about twenty feet in height and one foot in diameter. Although not considered a long-lived tree, ring countings have revealed an age in excess of 350 years for a few members of this species.

Pinyon pine has been observed growing in Grand Canyon National Park at elevations from 3,000 to 8,300 feet. The most vigorous growths, however, are found at elevations between 6,500 and 8,000 feet. . . . It is found interspersed with Utah juniper on the south and west exposures below altitudes where a less drought-resistant tree would not survive. . . .

While reproduction is limited at times by man, birds, and rodents accumulating hoards of nuts, the same agencies also aid in dissemination. Since the heavy seed has no well-defined seedwing by which it can be wind-borne, the above agents often cache the seeds in places suitable for germination and growth.

PINYON PINE NUTS

Ralph A. Redburn, Ranger Naturalist
October, 1931.

OUR ATTENTION HAS RECENTLY been attracted by the numerous little brown nuts which we see lying on the ground beneath the pinyon pine trees everywhere along the South Rim of the Grand Canyon. . . .

These are the nuts, called pinyon nuts or pine nuts, that have become famous because of their sweet white meat, which can readily be extracted from the shells. The shell is soft, and can be broken with the fingers or teeth. . . . In examining a large number of cones, I have found as many as thirty-four nuts in an individual. The average is about fifteen.

THE 1933 "PINE NUT" CROP

A. Russell Croft, Ranger Naturalist
September, 1932.

PINES BEAR TWO KINDS OF FLOWERS, commonly called cones. The male flowers, borne in lateral clusters principally on the lower two-thirds of the tree, produce pollen. Their function is completed as soon as the pollen is mature. The female flowers are small, conelike structures borne terminally, principally on the upper third of the tree. They contain the embryonic seeds and normally remain on the tree until mature, developing into the fruit. Two naked seeds are usually produced on the upper surface of each scale of the fruit (cone).

The 1933 fruit crop, estimated on the basis of the number of female flowers at the present time, will be reduced considerably before maturity by the following factors:

1. Failure to pollinate.
2. Failure to fertilize.
3. Mechanical injuries due to storms.
4. Consumption for food by animals.
5. Natural thinning.
6. Unknown causes.

Pinyon pines begin to produce male and female cones when they are about twenty-five years old. The cones are mere buds during their first season, and pollination takes place the following summer. Finally, female cones produce seeds, or nuts, in their third year. As noted here, they must survive many hazards to do so.

OH CEDAR!

Stephen B. Jones, Ranger Naturalist
May, 1930.

OFTEN THE RANGER NATURALIST . . . is asked about a certain tree and says: "That's a cedar." Then his informee replies: "Oh, I thought it was a juniper." Had the ranger-naturalist answered, as he often does: "That's a juniper," the questioner would have almost certainly replied: "Oh, I thought it was a cedar." So, an explanation is in order.

Strictly speaking, there are no cedars in America. If there is such a thing as a "true cedar," it is the cedar of the Old World, the Cedar of Lebanon. This is not native to America, but we have done our best to cover the deficiency by bestowing on at least a dozen trees the common name of cedar. In the northeast there is the *arborvitae*, known all over the country as the most common of ornamental trees. In the far northwest there is a giant cedar, a tree rivalling the redwood in size and graceful lines. Shingles of this "western red cedar" are sold all over the country, and to anyone who has seen one of these magnificent trees, the sight of a "western red cedar shingle" advertisement produces a sickening sensation and makes him wish that all roofs were slate or tile.

None of the aforementioned cedars occurs in Grand Canyon National Park. Our cedars are akin to those of much of the eastern United States. They are characterized by having berries. To the botanist, they are junipers. In the forest of the Coconino Plateau on the South Rim of the Canyon is an abundance of "Utah juniper." This drought-resisting tree grows far down into the Canyon, to the Redwall at least. On the North Rim, due to the greater altitude and consequent cooler, moister climate, Utah juniper is found only rarely, in such low places as Point Sublime and down in the tributary canyons. Another juniper, the "Rocky Mountain red cedar," takes its place as a forest tree, occurring along the rim of the Canyon and in considerable abundance in the vicinity of Grand Canyon Lodge.

MISCELLANY

Edwin D. McKee, Park Naturalist
November, 1931.

ALMOST THE ONLY TRACES OF ANIMAL LIFE found on a recent trip to Great Thumb Point were the droppings of coyotes, yet these were very numerous. Surprisingly enough, a large percentage of them contained numerous blue juniper berries, largely in undigested form.

WESTERN YELLOW PINE (PINUS PONDEROSA)

Glen E. Sturdevant, Park Naturalist
April, 1926.

THESE STRAIGHT-TRUNKED TREES are characterized by long, narrow crowns of hugely developed, bent branches. The trunk is smoothly cylindrical, with little taper until the large crown branches are reached. The bark of the older trees is marked by broad, russet-red plates, the surface of which is peculiar in that it is made up of small, concave scales. Younger trees up to two feet in diameter generally have a dark, red-brown or blackish, narrow-furrowed bark, and are called "blackjack" pines. The leaves or needles, varying from four to eleven inches in length, occur in bundles of threes. . . .

Maturing in two seasons, the cones measure 2-3/4 to 5-3/4 inches in length. The scale-tips of these massive cones are very thick, with stout, recurved prickles. The seeds contained therein are dull yellowish-brown in color, and resemble small navy beans in size. To each seed is attached a light brown seedwing some three-fourths of an inch in length. One of Nature's methods of perpetuating each form of life is evidenced by oftentimes finding these wind-borne seeds germinated considerable distance from any seed tree. . . .

Under proper conditions, the western yellow pine reaches an age of three hundred and fifty to five hundred years, with a diameter up to sixty inches. . . .

Recent investigations have shown that spacings of growth rings indicate the amount of rain for each year. The precipitation as evidenced by spacings of growth rings has coincided so accurately with the measured precipitation for the last score of years, that climatologists have lately availed themselves of this wonderful record kept by Nature for so long a period. . . .

The patterns of rings in trees of the Southwest are particularly distinctive, because the rainfall here varies so much from year to year. In 1901, the astronomer A.E. Douglass began studying tree-rings to determine whether they could be correlated to sunspots, hoping to use this information in forecasting the weather. Douglass used tree-rings to determine the climate of past centuries year by year, and established a record of weather fluctuations in this region reaching back centuries. This record has since been expanded and refined. Researchers as diverse as meteorologists, palaeobotanists, and archaeologists use it to reconstruct valuable information about the past (also see note on page 148).

Forests in the national parks are conserved for preservation, and cannot be valued because they are priceless. The large timbered areas in our National Parks are not only a great scenic asset, but in many cases they protect the sources of important rivers and watersheds, thereby preserving other scenic beauties. It is the duty of every American citizen to guard constantly against the encroachment on National Parks by commercial interests that would impair or destroy their forests and other wonders.

GAMBEL OAKS AT GRAND CANYON

Donald E. McHenry, Junior Naturalist
March, 1933.

THE MOST CHARACTERISTIC PLANT ASSOCIATION found in the Transition climatic Life Zone in Grand Canyon is that represented by the tall, sturdy, western yellow or ponderosa pines. To walk in the forest beneath the towering orange-yellow trunks of these trees is an experience recalling the stately pillars of ancient cathedrals, so open and free from undergrowth is the forest floor.

As if to add to the charm of this sylvan sanctuary, isolated groups of Gambel oaks are found judiciously scattered here and there among these pines. . . . They grow in colonies of a few to an average of about thirty individuals, and range in height from a foot or so to about fifteen feet.

We can hardly refer to Gambel oaks as individuals, because of their peculiar communal life. Rarely does one find these trees growing alone. The colonial habit which they have developed is the result of an interesting, if not unusual type of root system. Instead of producing the tap root commonly found in members of its family, the Gambel oak develops an elaborate, horizontal, underground root system, in some ways similar in growth habit to the rhizome of a fern. This horizontal root system grows in several directions from the "parent" tree of the colony, and from these "runners" new aerial shoots arise at intervals. In this manner, all the individuals of a colony continue to live attached to a common, horizontal root system. Beneath each tree, a limited secondary root system develops. One would conclude that, provided with sufficient tools and manpower, an entire colony of Gambel oaks could be dug up and transplanted *en toto*.

QUAKING ASPEN AT GRAND CANYON

Donald E. McHenry, Junior Naturalist
December, 1932.

ONE CAN NEVER FORGET THE NORTH RIM of the Grand Canyon in autumn. Driving along its enchanted scenic highways, one's fancy is intrigued by the varied colors of the turning aspen trees set deep in the somber green of the dense forest of tall spruces and firs. They appear almost to be patches of sunlight hurriedly left behind by a sun too eager to sink to rest after its day's journey. . . .

The relationship of the aspen to our common cottonwood tree is suggested in the habit of the female trees giving off

spring showers of cottonlike material, which bears the fruit. At times this is so conspicuous that the immediate territory seems to be enjoying a light, warm, snowstorm.

Populus tremuloides, or quaking aspen, gets its name from the trembling habit of its leaves in the slightest breeze. This activity is caused by the manner in which the petiole of the leaf is attached to the leaf blade. At the point of attachment, the petiole is compressed at right angles to the plane of the leaf blade, thus allowing it to give with the slightest air current.

QUAKING ASPEN—ITS FUTURE IN THE PARK

Donald E. McHenry, Junior Naturalist
January, 1935.

THE ASPEN, A SUB-CLIMAX SPECIES in our forest on the North Rim, is just one of several steps of plant succession in the natural reforestation of burntover areas in this region. The presence of aspen trees in such great numbers on the North Rim, where it seems to be an indicator of former forest fires, bears witness to the extent of the early fires in this region. That there were such forest fires is a fact which is supported by statements of some of the "old-timers" in southern Utah, the country a little to the north of the North Rim. Nate Adams, one of these early pioneers still living in Kanab in southeastern Utah, tells how in the pioneer days of this community, the inhabitants would frequently look to the south to see great clouds of smoke rolling over the Kaibab Plateau on the North Rim of the Grand Canyon. This smoke would be almost continuous from early spring until late autumn. . . . It is supposed . . . that many of these fires were caused by lightning, for that is still the case today. . . .

Everywhere that the ground was swept clean by such fires, this made way for a series of changes which eventually made possible the present beautiful stands of quaking aspen in the Kaibab forest. Much of this took place in the days before this area was made a national reserve or a national forest.

Today, now that modern methods of fire protection are maintained in this forest by both the National Park Service and the National Forest Service, the number of fires and the extent of the areas destroyed by them have been reduced to a negligible quantity. Under this present influence, there is a greater chance for natural reforestation to progress along lines of normal development. This involves an interesting plant succession which obviously has been in progress for some time. With fewer interruptions by forest fires, this succession will normally proceed to a climax vegetation. The aspen is not a climax but a subclimax tree in this forest. It is obvious that at best it can be considered but a temporary tree. In the changes which are bound to occur in this plant succession, it is evident that the aspen will finally decrease as the climax evergreens crowd it out. Many evidences that this is now in progress on the North Rim can be found. . . .

DOES MISTLETOE KILL THE TREES AT GRAND CANYON?

Donald E. McHenry, Junior Naturalist
August, 1934.

WHEN THE EARLY DRUIDS venerated the mistletoe as a sacred or mystic plant, it was because this strange form of vegetation was found growing midway between heaven and earth but, as they said, really belonged to neither. Little did they suspect that this interesting plant, far from being of the gods, was actually a brigand exhausting the vitality of the very support which made possible its exalted position and gave it its semi-divine reputation.

Not in the same mystic sense, but nonetheless with considerable interest, do the modern visitors to Grand Canyon National Park view the yellowish-green clumps of mistletoe which dot some of our evergreen trees. . . . As one discovers these parasites and then finds a dead tree near by, he frequently wonders whether or not the tree has been killed by mistletoe. Such a conclusion seems especially probable if the dead tree has the characteristic scrubby growth known as "witch's broom" on its branches—the adventitious growth induced by the hemiparasitic mistletoe. . . .

The writer holds the opinion that in the majority of cases where trees infected with mistletoe have been killed, their death is due not to this parasite alone but to the presence of secondary insect infestation; therefore, no effective measure for the control of the spread of mistletoe is being followed.

CHAPTER V
Invertebrates, Reptiles, Amphibians, and Fish

SOME BEETLES OF GRAND CANYON

Clyde C. Searl, Ranger Naturalist
April, 1931.

A FEW DAYS AGO, while looking over one of the wild-flower gardens at the Yavapai Observation Station, a steady rapid buzz caught my attention. . . . It was a beetle, and from its action in flight I knew that it was a Scarab. . . .

SCARAB

There is another interesting beetle, common to the warm dry parts of the western United States, found at Grand Canyon. It belongs to the family *Tenebrionidae*, and has a number of common names. The darkling beetle seems to be the most appropriate, although it is also known as the pinacate bug or just stinkbug. The last two common names are misleading, inasmuch as beetles are not bugs. . . .

Most darkling beetles are clumsy fellows, and very slow moving. One group, the *Eleodes*, when disturbed will elevate the hind part of the body, and emit an offensive-smelling, oily fluid.

PINACATE BUG

AN INTERESTING BUG

Clyde C. Searl, Ranger Naturalist
May, 1931.

SINCE THE FIRST WEEK IN MAY, the trees and shrubs around Grand Canyon Village have harbored myriads of a noisy type of insect. It is a cicada, erroneously called a locust by many people. (The true locust is a member of the grasshopper group.) Although the cicada has been practically unknown at Grand Canyon Village for several years past, this year it appears to be very abundant, and keeps up a constant clicking in every tree.

CICADA

. . . [I]t is believed that cicadas have the longest life cycle of any insect. . . . The period of metamorphosis, however, depends largely upon environment. In the warm southern range of the "seventeen-year locust," the adult stage is reached in about ten years.

CRICKET NOTES

Earl W. Count, Ranger Naturalist
August, 1929.

I HAD JUST PUT OUT THE BONFIRE at the tourist camp after the evening lecture and was walking home, when near me beside the gravel path I heard a fiddle. With flashlight and a very little persistence, I located the musician in a crack between two rocks that lined the path.

Imagine a person standing on his head, and bracing himself

against a wall while sawing one coattail with the other, and you can picture the bizarre attitude the musician—a little cricket—was in. . . . The motion was similar to the spreading of a fan; the wings spread, never quite separated, and then slid together again. Every time they spread, they trembled violently, and this produced the rasp.

DRAGONFLIES AT GRAND CANYON

Clyde C. Searl, Ranger Naturalist
December, 1931.

SEVERAL KINDS AND VARIETIES OF DRAGONFLIES, and their relatives the damselflies, are found in the Grand Canyon region. Along Bright Angel Creek they are especially numerous, and many have been collected below Grand Canyon Village at Indian Gardens where there is a small stream suitable for life in the immature form. They have long, slender, and very stiff bodies of metallic colors [such] as steel blue, purple, green, bronze, copper, and silver-white. Their four long, silver-gauze wings are beautifully veined, and are often

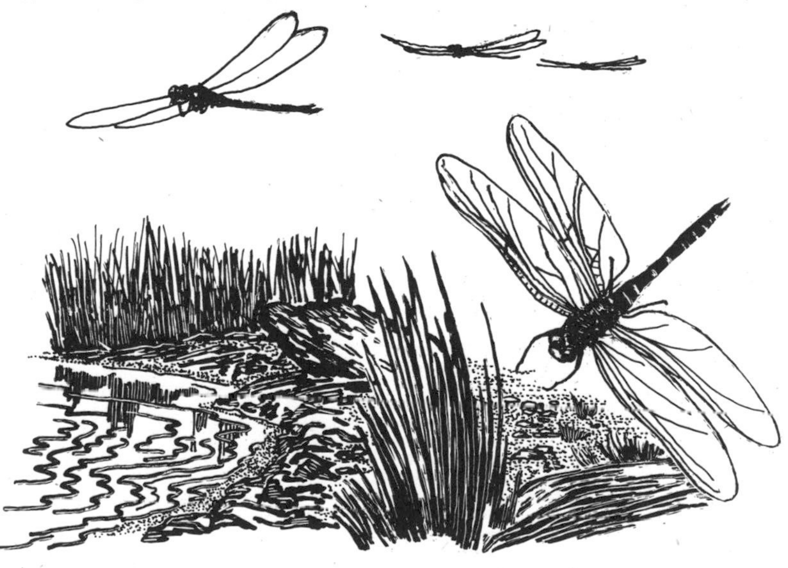

spotted with white or amber or ruby-colored patches. Their eyes are literally like jewels, and stand out in front of their weird faces. . . .

The larvae of dragonflies are not worms or grubs as are the larvae of beetles, moths, and butterflies, but they are imperfect insects similar to the younger stages of the grasshopper. They are called nymphs and they live in the mud of streams, clinging to the roots of plants and feeding upon mosquito larvae, tadpoles, caddis worms, mayfly larvae, and countless other denizens of stream and pond beds.

VANDALS OF THE SAND

Clyde C. Searl, Ranger Naturalist
March, 1932.

OFTEN AT NIGHT AROUND CAMPFIRES, or hovering about electric lights or lanterns, is seen a clumsy insect similar in general appearance to a dragonfly, but differing from that insect in that it flaps all four wings in flight. Time and again, the writer has invited condemnation and doubt by telling people that this insect, which is fairly common in the Grand Canyon region, is an ant lion. It is difficult to believe that such a large creature can be the mature form of the common little ant lion or doodlebug with which people are familiar in the larval stage. . . .

The larva ant lion has six digging legs, and its mouth is like a mousetrap. It excavates a conical-shaped hole in the sand, the average size of which is about an inch deep and approximately an inch and a half across. Partly concealed beneath the sand at the apex of the cone it awaits, eyes on the lookout and jaws ready to snap the prey. If any little insect creeper or spider comes along in search of food and falls into the pit, sliding to the bottom, it is snatched by the ant lion.

THE POLYPHEMUS MOTH

Edwin D. McKee, Ranger Naturalist
July, 1928.

ADAPTABILITY TO A VARIETY OF CONDITIONS—especially those of climate and food supply—must undoubtedly be recognized as very significant factors in the success of animal types. . . .

The recent discovery in the Grand Canyon National Park of the presence of *Telia Polyphemus*, beautiful member of the giant forest moths, seems to suggest this feature. . . . This beautiful moth certainly has many enemies—parasitic, feathered, and human—yet it still appears to be a very successful competitor in the game of life. . . . In the Grand Canyon, where it was recently found in the Transition Zone of the south side, its larvae probably feed upon the white oak or perhaps even on the yellow pine. In any case, it is significant that this beautiful silk-spinner has found food and thrived where near relatives, who are apparently on an equal basis yet unable to adapt themselves to new foods and conditions, have failed.

TELIA POLYPHEMUS

THE PAPILIO TRIBE OF BUTTERFLIES

Edwin D. McKee, Ranger Naturalist
July, 1927.

THE BELIEF THAT GRAND CANYON NATIONAL PARK is blessed with a bountiful representation of Nature's painted, soaring creatures—the butterflies—is ably supported by members of the genus *Papilio* or swallowtail, America's largest butterflies. From this single group have recently been seen and collected three different species which are the representatives of a like number of distinct life zones, and which between them range over the entire territory formed by the Canyon's depth. Every one of these butterflies is exceptionally distinctive by its huge size—having a wingspread of more than three inches—and by its long tail and brilliant colors.

Starting in the Inner or Granite Gorge. . . . Here is seen in great abundance the gaudy pipevine swallowtail with beautiful, iridescent wings of green and black. It is a most conspicuous figure as it flits about among the cottonwoods, where it lends much color to the scene. . . .

Typical of the Upper Sonoran itself is the beautiful but little known species *Papilio hollandi*, a butterfly of metallic blue interspersed with brilliant yellow.

Then again passing higher . . . the mighty two-tailed swallowtail. One specimen collected from this section had a wing expansion of five and one-half inches—even greater than the type dimensions—and all are of a huge size. There is little doubt but that this remarkable size, coupled with the brilliant, yellow-and black markings and the double tails of the lower wings, more closely resembles some wonderful tropical bird than a mere butterfly. Thus in the Transition Zone—the upper walls of the Canyon—we have a real king of butterflies.

SCORPION VS. TARANTULA

Barbara Hastings McKee
April, 1932.

TWO OF THE DENIZENS of the Grand Canyon region, which have received notoriety from their bad reputation of inflicting painful, poisonous stings, are the scorpion and the tarantula. While these creatures are not so abundant that most visitors to the National Park ever see them, they are fairly common in their respective life zones.

The scorpion found at Grand Canyon is most abundant at the bottom of the gorge, in the warmer Lower Sonoran Zone. A few specimens have been found on the South Rim, however. This species often reaches a length of six inches, though the average is a little less than this. There is no case on record here of a fatality resulting from the sting of the scorpion, but in several instances a very painful wound has been inflicted. . . .

The tarantulas of this region are seen very frequently during their mating season—September—when large, black, hairy fellows are often noticed as they walk across the roads. During other times of the year they are little in evidence. . . . As far as I can ascertain, no one in Grand Canyon has ever been bitten by one of these large spiders, so I do not know how painful or what the effects of such an experience would be.

HORNED TOADS

Stephen B. Jones, Ranger Naturalist
September, 1929.

AUGUST WAS HORNED TOAD MONTH on the North Rim. In this month, the pine and aspen woods were a big nursery for infant "hornies." The young of these interesting lizards are born alive. The females become very big just before the young are born, and in August these nearly spherical females were abundant in the woods. Oddly enough, the horned toads of the park are not found among the rocks as are most lizards, nor down in the Canyon, but seem to live and die in the shade of the forested plateau. . . .

I have kept several horned toads in a pen for a month or so, and have watched them feed—for that is about all a horned toad does. The pen was a circle of sheet metal, and was built around an anthill. At first they showed an aversion to feeding while I was watching them, but hunger overcame their suspicions and I have witnessed the end of many an ant. . . .

I have exhibited horned toads at Grand Canyon Lodge many times, and I seldom find anyone, man or woman, who has any aversion to these curious reptiles. Perhaps it is the belief that they are toads instead of lizards that makes people like them. It is a delight to catch one that has just shed his skin and to have people who have always shuddered at the very mention of reptiles exclaim at the colors of his velvety back, or to "put him to sleep" by rubbing his head and to hear people say: "How cute!" when an hour before, considering lizards abstractly, they would have said: "It makes me sick to look at them." In fact, one of my problems is to keep tourists from running off with our horned toads, so attractive are they. Aside from the difficulty of feeding an animal that seems to want living prey, we need the horned toads in the forest, for they are one of our indispensable checks on insect life.

A "REPTILE STORY"

A. Russell Croft, Ranger Naturalist
November, 1932.

"REPTILE STORIES," LIKE "BEAR STORIES," constitute a group of so-called experiences, questionable statements, and proverbial hearsay. Most every individual has a supply of such stories which he brings to his rescue when good fellows exchange "whoppers" on appropriate occasions. . . .

One such story concerns the horned lizard, the Grand Canyon species of which is commonly called the shorthorned horned toad. The story is: "Occasional specimens of horned lizard have been seen to eject a thin stream of blood from the corner of the eye, taking place when the specimen has been disturbed or annoyed. . . ."

Early in June, 1932, one of a party of hikers being conducted on a field trip by the author picked up a horned lizard, and the much-questioned stream of blood was ejected from the left eye with considerable force and without the slightest provocation. . . .

The cause of this unusual reaction is not known. Many horned lizards have been subjected to various kinds of stimuli in an effort to induce the reaction, but it seems that no one has been rewarded with a demonstration in response to such attempts. . . .

At any rate, this is one "Reptile Story" which is true.

THE BLUEBELLIED LIZARD

Edwin D. McKee, Ranger Naturalist
August, 1928.

THE BLUEBELLIED LIZARD, or *Sceloporus elongatus*, is undoubtedly the most abundant and most widely distributed reptile in the Grand Canyon National Park. Apparently, it is sufficiently versatile to exist under all climatic conditions represented in this region, and readily to adapt itself to quite varied environments. . . .

At first sight—whether among the gray rocks forming the Canyon's rim or on the perpendicular surfaces of some black schists down in the Canyon's depths—the bluebellied lizard appears to be a dull, uninteresting creature lacking entirely in beauty. A closer examination, however, soon shows this thought to be entirely erroneous. The scales of the back actually form a very beautiful network design of a rich black color intermingled with a pure gray background. . . . Deep blue patches are found on the flanks and one on each side of the throat of both males and females, thus making a rather colorful creature.

Sceloporus, the scientific name of the genus, is one applied to a large group commonly known as "swifts" or "fence" lizards.

Today, most field guides refer to members of this genus as "spiny lizards." This particular species is now called a "northern plateau lizard," *Sceloporus undulatus elongatus*.

THE CHUCKWALLA

Barbara Hastings, Ranger Naturalist
May, 1929.

DOWN IN THE BOTTOM OF THE GRAND CANYON and over the low, hot deserts lives a large, dark, rough, rock lizard related to the iguanas. This lizard—the chuckwalla—is one of the largest found in the United States, second only in size to the gila monster, and for untold ages it has furnished a choice food for desert Indians. Many a prospector and desert wayfarer has made a meal on one of these big lizards, and found its flesh palatable and wholesome.

Recently while following a faint trail along the Colorado River near Phantom Ranch, I was with Mr. Vernon Bailey of the U.S. Biological Survey when he secured a large chuckwalla. . . . Its stomach was carefully examined. . . . The large flowerheads of three species of milky-juiced composites had been eaten to the number of one hundred and eighteen, and three fresh flowers of the yellow bean bush. These represented the breakfast of the chuckwalla.

LIZARD EAT LIZARD

Donald E. McHenry, Junior Naturalist
June, 1934.

ON OCCASION, VISITORS ABSORBED in viewing the almost unbelievable, unreal spectacle of the Grand Canyon will have their attention diverted for a moment from this sublime scene to a micro-drama being enacted at their very feet.

One such drama took place at Yavapai Point, just outside the Observation Station at noon on April 27. The arena was the crevice of a rock. Upon the occasion, about a dozen peo-

A Striped Swift Swallowing Uta

ple forgot such an important thing as lunch. One can eat lunch any day, but it is not often that the average person is privileged to watch a striped swift gulping down an Arizona tree uta. So great was the strain upon the sympathies of one of the female members of the group of observers that she tried to discourage further descent of the uta into the interior of the swift. But the swift was so intent upon the engulfing that it paid not the least attention to the nervous advances, and kept right on gulping. . . .

ODDS AND ENDS

March, 1931.

DURING A WARM SPELL the first part of the month of March, two lizards of the genus *Uta* were seen daily disporting themselves on the walk of Yavapai Observation Station. Both were very young lizards, and it is highly possible that experience had not yet taught them that it was indiscreet to come out until warm weather was surely with us. The present cold spell has taught them that two or three warm days do not mean that summer is here.

April, 1931.

THE GRACEFUL LITTLE PATCHNOSE SNAKE was found near Panorama Point on the Kaibab Trail, April 13. This is the second record of this typically southwestern reptile from the Grand Canyon National Park.

July, 1929.

TWO SPECIMENS of a brilliant red, black, and white kingsnake have recently been found by Ranger Ed Laws at the high elevations of the North Rim.

September, 1929.

A BIG SCALY LIZARD (*Sceloporus magister*) was recently observed on Cedar Ridge, about a thousand feet from the rim on the Kaibab Trail. As far as known, these reptiles have not previously been recorded above the Inner Gorge of the Grand Canyon, though they are very abundant along the Colorado River and side creeks of this region.

THE GRAND CANYON RATTLESNAKE

Edwin D. McKee, Park Naturalist
April, 1930.

AT LAST Grand Canyon has a namesake! In the winter just past, Mr. L.M. Klauber of the San Diego Museum of Natural History has completed a careful study of western rattle-snakes of the species *Crotalus confluentus*. In collecting and sending to Mr. Klauber some six or seven specimens of the rattler of this species, which is found uncommonly in Grand Canyon, the naturalist staff of the park little realized that the creation of a new subspecies bearing the name of Grand Canyon Rattlesnake would result.

The Grand Canyon rattlesnake (*Crotalus confluentus abyssus*) is a typically pink or salmon-colored reptile with very indistinct markings in the adult form. It is larger than most rattlers of this group, and so far as known, is confined in range to the inside of Grand Canyon.

The name of this snake has been revised to *Crotalus viridis abyssus*.

RATTLESNAKES ON THE CANYON RIM

Donald E. McHenry, Junior Naturalist
November, 1933.

MUCH INTEREST HAS BEEN SHOWN by park visitors over the possible presence of rattlesnakes on the North Rim of the Grand Canyon. Every once in a while, some panic-stricken person reports having killed such a snake. Such persons frequently describe just how the "rattlesnake" rattled when they approached him unexpectedly. These people appear disappointed when they learn that their "rattler" is none other than the harmless and decidedly beneficial bull or Utah gopher snake, a snake frequently found on this rim, and that the rattling which they heard was nothing but the hissing of this snake which, in their excitement, they mistook for evidence of real danger.

A GOPHER-SNAKE LUNCHES

Earl W. Count, Ranger Naturalist
July, 1931.

AS I WAS LECTURING to a large group of people at the Yavapai Station recently, a series of squeaks and something of a commotion nearly caused me to lose part of my audience. When I had come to a close, most of us gathered in a corner of the porch to watch a forty-four and one-half inch gophersnake "reap the benefits of the chase."

A good-sized packrat was on its way down the throat of the snake; head first, flattened, with hind feet spread. It was, of course, quite dead by now. Occasionally, the snake would writhe, bringing two or three loops up over that part of its body which was enlarged by the addition of the rat. Possibly the squeezing helped force the prey down. Over the enlarged part of the snake's body passed waves of contraction from the rear forward; these being seen when the loops were not covering the body. The food thus moved to the rear on the principle of pulling a drawstring into the hemmed neck of a sack. Then loops would be flung forward over the rat, repeatedly burying the head of the snake at the same time. This action stretched the rat and rounded it into a more compact form. . . .

It is a perpetual source of stupefaction to witnesses of this feat to see that mouth stretch so enormously; an explanation therefore may not be amiss. The bones in the jaws of the snake are not knit into a firm structure as in the human. . . . Thus the snake jaw can drop farther, and can expand sidewise at both ends to form a truly yawning cavity.

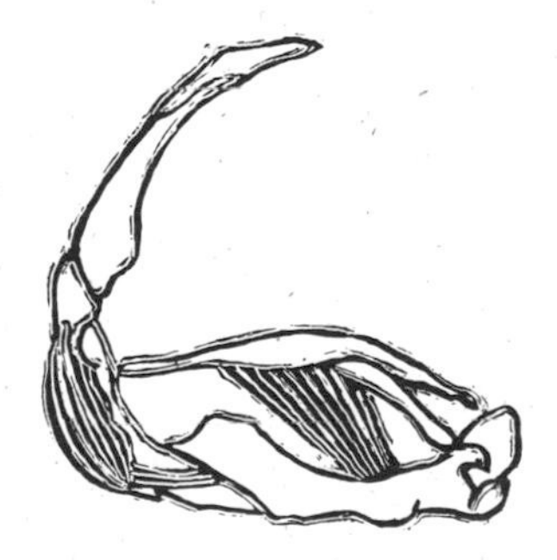
Diagram of Snake Head

A meat-eating animal possessed of legs may use them for holding and manipulating its prey while tearing it to pieces. The flexible head of a snake may be part of Nature's ingenious way for compensating an animal which she has bereft of those important appendages. It is indeed a versatile creature that can run, climb, swim, hunt, fight, and eat efficiently without their aid.

NOTES ON GRAND CANYON AMPHIBIANS

Charles M. Bogert, Ranger Naturalist
March, 1933.

WITHIN THE LIMITS of Grand Canyon National Park, only four species have been recorded to date, although there is a strong possibility that two or three others will be discovered here. Environment alone seems not to be the only factor governing the distribution of amphibians, as the introduction of new species into some areas has demonstrated. It is interesting to conjecture regarding the presence of amphibians at desert oases, the Rocky Mountain toad, for instance. Have these been carried there by other animals such as birds, or are they remnants possibly surviving from a time when the entire area was within a moist climate?

The only tailed amphibian in Arizona, the tiger salamander, called *axolotl* in the larval stage, is known from the tanks on the South Rim and from Greenland Lake on the North Rim. The larvae are rather common in these pools of water, but to date I believe only two adults have been found.

Two other amphibians known in the Park are more numerous. The Sonoran tree toad is common about permanent shady pools in the canyon bottoms. This species was observed to be especially common around the pools below the falls in Havasu Canyon.

But the spotted toad is the commonest of the three. During rains they come forth in great numbers, and while they are more prevalent in the Canyon bottoms at such places as Indian Gardens, Burro Springs, etc., they range up near and perhaps to the South Rim. Between rains, refuge is sought in crevices in the rocks, or at places where there is a slight seepage. One hot day in July, a barrel of water near the stable at the mouth of Bright Angel Creek was overturned, and nineteen toads were found beneath it. . . .

What is apparently the first occurrence of the spadefoot toad to be reported from within the limits of Grand Canyon

National Park was published in Grand Canyon Nature Notes for October, 1932. Mr. Wallace F. Wood found the larvae and newly metamorphosed young of this toad in Greenland Lake on the North Rim, July 1, 1932.

TROUT PROPAGATION IN GRAND CANYON NATIONAL PARK

Robert B. Williamson, Park Ranger, and
Carol F. Tyler, Clerk-Stenographer
May, 1932.

THE PROPAGATION OF FISH in Grand Canyon National Park has been carried on for a number of years, and though there is no record of the species of fish or of the number planted prior to 1920, it is known that the Forest Service made some planting in the more accessible streams prior to the creation of the National Park in 1919.

Within the park there are five streams suitable for trout propagation. These are Bright Angel Creek, Shinumo Creek, Tapeats Creek (Thunder River), Clear Creek, and Havasu Creek. . . .

All of the streams above mentioned are tributaries of the Colorado River, and with the exception of Havasu Creek, flow into the Colorado River from the north.

PLANTING FISH EGGS IN CLEAR CREEK

P.P. Patraw, Assistant Superintendent
February, 1934.

AFTER A STUDY HAD BEEN MADE of the rate of flow of the stream and of types and abundance of natural foods, it was determined that Clear Creek is a stream suitable for trout. An order was placed on the government fish hatchery at Leadville, Colorado, for twenty-five thousand eyed eggs of eastern brook trout. The eggs arrived by express on Tuesday morning, and were transferred from their shipping cases into two, manpack-carrying cases. . . .

Two days previously, rangers had gone to Clear Creek to prepare the beds for the plant. Locations for beds are selected where the stream flows in a normal swift current, having no eddies or pools, and the beds are prepared by raking so that the silt is disturbed for the stream to carry it away, leaving only clean gravel.

Loading Cans of Fish on Mules in Preparation for Fish Planting in the Canyon

The following morning, after replenishing the ice in the cases, we set out for Clear Creek. Two of us carried the cases and the other two had much lighter knapsacks containing provisions, camera, etc. We alternated carrying light and heavy loads. Our route was up Bright Angel Creek a mile, then the steep climb up the granite wall and Tapeats sandstone, twelve hundred feet higher in elevation to the Tonto platform, over the Tonto heading four small canyons at the base of Zoroaster Temple to Clear Creek Canyon, where we dropped down to the creek and went upstream to our camp under an overhanging cliff, in the midst of numerous ruins of prehistoric dwellings. It was a relief to take off the packs which we had been carrying on our backs for six or seven hours, and which had seemed to grow heavier each hour. The sun had been hot, and the only shade was such as a lizard might have found large enough to use. It would be excellent reducing exercise to carry a heavy pack up and down Canyon walls and over the hot plateau if it weren't for the enormous quantity of food and water one demands at the end of the day. . . .

In making a plant, the previously-prepared bed is first raked to make sure that no silt has been redeposited since the original preparation. The planting board, a hinged affair having two metal wings about twelve inches square, is opened to a right angle and placed in the stream with the angle upstream. The board prevents the current from sweeping over the spot in which the eggs are to be deposited, so that the eggs will not be washed away. A small hole is scraped in the gravel, about two hundred eggs are placed in it, and the gravel is replaced to cover the eggs.

CHAPTER VI
Birds

WATER OUZEL

Glen E. Sturdevant, Park Naturalist
April, 1926.

THESE CURIOUS MEMBERS of birdlife have been cited by Darwin as one of the exponents in proving the theory that made him famous. . . . At some remote period, probably hundreds of generations of birdlife age, a bird which was perhaps the common and more generalized ancestor of our thrushes, warblers, wrens, etc., had spread widely over the great northern continent . . . this stock gave rise to numerous varieties adapted to special conditions of life. Among these, some took to feeding on the borders of clear streams, picking out such larvae and mollusks as they could reach in shallow water. When food became scarce, they would attempt to pick them out of deeper and deeper water. While doing this in cold weather many would become frozen and starved. But any which possessed denser and more hairy plumage than usual, which was able to keep out the water, would survive; and thus a race might be formed which would depend more and more on this kind of food. Following up the mountainous streams, where the velocity of the water was great enough to prevent it being easily frozen over, they could live there during the winter protected from their enemies, and with ample shelter for their nests and young. Further adaptations occurred until the wonderful power of diving and flying underwater was acquired by a true land bird. . . .

The accepted common name for this bird has changed from "water ouzel" to "American dipper." (Its Latin name is *Cinclus mexicanus*.)

The feet are well formed for walking. The strongly curved claws aid them in retaining their grasp on the rocks while feeding underwater. The food consists of waterbeetles, caddis worms, and other insect larvae, as well as numerous small, freshwater shells. With the aid of their short, muscular wings for power, they are able to propel themselves about underwater without the customary aid of webbed feet. According to the best observers, this extraordinary power of flying underwater is their process of diving in search of prey.

OBSERVATIONS

August, 1928.

TWO WATER OUZELS' NESTS were found recently on ledges in the sheer walls of the Box Canyon, Bright Angel Creek. In both cases, they were located about four feet above the streambed. One nest, which was examined by wading the stream, proved to be built mostly of lichens and lined inside with soft grasses. It contained five pure white eggs.

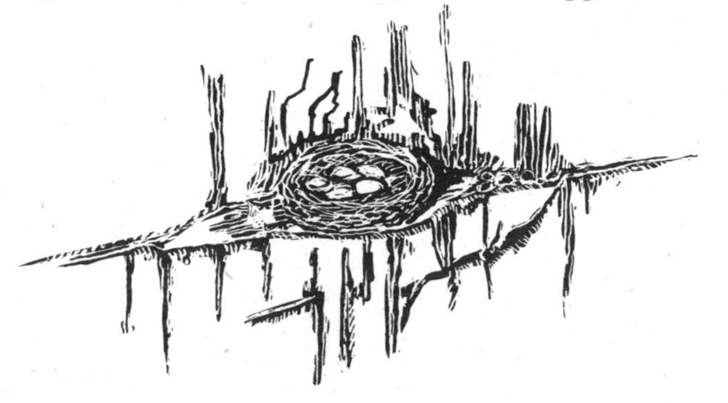

REDSHAFTED FLICKER NESTS ON CANYON RIM

Glen E. Sturdevant, Park Naturalist
May, 1928.

AT LEAST ONE PAIR of redshafted flickers has decided that the Grand Canyon is an ideal spot to propagate their kind.

They have selected a home in a dead pinyon pine near the Yavapai Point footpath. The tree has four old holes and one recently bored hole on the east side. The fresh hole in the tree suggested that some member of the woodpecker family had a home there. After a few knocks, Mrs. Flicker announced herself by flying out of the hole and alighting in a nearby tree. Within a short time, she returned to the tree and re-entered her home.

AVIAN CLIFF-DWELLERS

Earl W. Count, Ranger Naturalist
November, 1929.

TOURISTS WHO VISIT US during the summer are always privileged to view quantities of very lively speedsters swooping from the rim of the Canyon. It is obvious that some are swallows, but some are not. We have here one of those strange associations that stud the book of nature; for the northern violet-green swallow is of the order of perching-birds (*Passeriformes*), while the white-throated swift is a relative of the hummingbird (order *Apodiformes*). . . .

The swallows, with their broader and shorter wings, flutter much more than the swifts; nor is their flight as rapid. Of evenings a short way back from the rim, you may see swallows competing with bats for the insects dancing in the air, and necessarily following a very erratic course.

The swift, on the other hand, may startle you when you stand near the rim as he whistles past at dizzying speed. Dr. H.C. Bryant has compared this bird to a crossbow. His wings form a beautiful arc, and his gondola-body rests between them. His flight is a long shot, or dive in one direction; then comes a sharp wheel and another dive. He possesses the unique trick of beating his wings alternately instead of together, which causes a not ungraceful "wobble" in the flight.

You may, if lucky, see the bottle-green on back and wings of the violet-green swallow; if still more lucky, you may see the bronzy hue on crown and neck, or a violet collarband on the nape; and the white of the rump almost meets on the back. The swift has to make up in spectacular flight for a lack of protective color; he is blackish on upper parts and sides, white on throat and breast, and has white patches on wings and rump.

BIRDING IN GRAND CANYON

Randolph Jenks, Curator of Ornithology
Museum of Northern Arizona
June, 1931.

I ARRIVED JUST BEFORE SUNSET at Yaki Point on the South Rim of Grand Canyon. . . . A nighthawk was flying in and out among the swifts, getting its full share of the evening meal. From a pine tree just back of the rim, a pair of long-crested [Stellers] jays cocked their heads at me and scolded furiously. They were defying me to approach their secret haunt, near which I suspect they had a nest. . . . I turned my back to the jays and started down the Kaibab Trail. A friendly chickadee bade me "good luck" from a juniper. He scarcely had time to open his bill, so anxious was he to eat every insect on the branch of that tree as he clung there, upside down.

On reaching the Tonto Platform, I saw a pair of western lark sparrows eating seeds at the base of a large tuft of grass. When I approached they flew to a rocky ledge nearby, and uttered a few musical notes. At that moment, a rock wren started to scold them loudly and so made them fly away. It was almost dark. . . . A poor-will called constantly and mysteriously from the overhanging rock ledges which were surrounded by junipers. At the lower edge of the Tonto Platform, from a mesquite bush a mockingbird continually repeated snatches of the songs of several birds which it probably had heard during the day. . . .

Early the following morning at Phantom Ranch, I was awakened by the beautiful, shrill call of the canyon wren. Many kinds of warblers were singing in the bushes and cottonwood trees. . . . In the mesquite and catsclaw bushes, western gnatcatchers were nervously searching for insects. I heard Gambel quail calling from the edge of the bluffs. . . . I watched a solitary sandpiper feeding along the bank of the stream.

Shortly after daybreak on Sunday, I left the Ranch expecting to reach the South Rim by noon. . . .

When I reached Indian Gardens, I saw more birds than in any other place on the trip. Four or five chats appeared above the thick brushy growth, and some of them sang. . . . A pair of small flycatchers were busily occupied building a nest near the trail. Lazuli buntings were mating, the male displaying his beautiful feathers before his admiring lover.

THE TURKEY BUZZARD

Glen E. Sturdevant, Park Naturalist
December, 1926.

ACCORDED ADMIRATION FOR THE GRACEFUL manner in which he maneuvers his ponderous body through the air, rather than the food he chooses to eat, permits an introduction to the turkey buzzard.

With a few graceful turns in the air, the bird is seen to rise upwards and upwards. Whether it is due to air currents within the Canyon or some muscular effort too slight for the eye to catch, it is impossible to state. . . .

Its food consists of carrion. Any animal that succumbs to death in the Grand Canyon region has not long to wait until a score or more of dark bodies are seen circling warily overhead. Only when assured apparently that the silent form beneath is not playing "possum," will these birds alight for their natural food. . . .

The head of the buzzard is practically bare of feathers. This corrugated skin of the head resembles the crimson skin on a turkey's head. Upon the ground the large bird is often mistaken for a turkey—hence the name turkey buzzard or turkey vulture.

The nest occurs in protected places beneath large overhanging rocks, or in caverns in the walls of the Canyon. The two eggs are deposited in a scooped-out place in the earth. The young are a downy white with blackish heads. Upon approaching them, they send forth a hissing noise not unlike a tame turkey hen on a nest. . . .

The buzzard is harmless when left alone. Any enemies are adequately coped with, however, in a singular manner. When attacked, he resorts to the vile practice of disgorging the putrid contents of his last meal, which is fully as effective as the defensive tactics of the skunk.

The accepted common name for this bird today is "Turkey *vulture*."

THE GATHERING OF THE JAY CLAN

Earl W. Count, Ranger Naturalist
September, 1929.

ABOUT THE END OF AUGUST, THE BRILLIANT, long-crested [Stellers] jay, who all summer relieves the monotony of the pinyon pines, was overshadowed by the enthusiastic horde of pinyon jays gathering for migration. For a few days these self-confident and garrulous picnickers tramped the forest floor at Yavapai Point and charged from tree to tree, making all sorts of dogmatic and forceful comments about things in general. It is eternally amusing to see one of them walk up to a hanging pinyon cone, eye it from that side and this, and open that scissorlike beak to clamp onto an obviously oversize mouthful. . . . Or, this jay pecks and pecks, only to smear his beak with the gum oozing from the cone; whereupon he retires for a siege of whetting. If he secures a decent bite, say a pinyon nut or a whole cone, he has the usual jay-method of whacking it to pieces on the limb of a tree.

The pinyon jay wears the sky-blue of the French army, but is slightly lighter underneath, especially on the throat. He has no crest, and the crown of his head is a brighter blue than the rest of him.

Mexican Spotted Owl

THE HERMIT OF HORN CREEK

Edwin D. McKee, Park Naturalist
February, 1933.

IN LATE OCTOBER, 1932, another Mexican spotted owl was found in Grand Canyon—apparently the second record from the Canyon and the third from northern Arizona. . . . Dr. John Maxson . . . writes the following description of the occurrence:

> "I was amazed that it showed little inclination to desert the rocky crag upon which I surprised it. Both the owl and I were startled; the owl because of the unprece-

dented interruption of the solitude of Horn Creek, and I because my footholds and handholds were very precarious. I set up my tripod in order to focus exactly and he became somewhat perturbed, ruffling his feathers lightly but keeping his eyes shut. He, of course, faced in my direction constantly and stayed at a distance of about ten feet. Not until Dr. Campbell, who was with me, came up on the cliff back of him did he become really disturbed. Then he could not watch both of us at once, but had to turn his head hither and yon to keep track of us. At the coincidence of movement by both of us, he ruffled his feathers till he was oval, opened his eyes very wide, and had a thorough evacuation. As we left, he resumed his sleep."

Although sightings are rare, the Grand Canyon is a recognized habitat for the Mexican Spotted Owl.

A WINTER RESIDENT

Glen E. Sturdevant, Park Naturalist
March, 1927.

WHAT CAUSES THE ROBIN to remain away from his warm southern home during the winter? Some suggest that the ones remaining are old birds inured to cold and privation, and prefer to cast their lot in the great struggle for existence by remaining at the place of their summer home rather than making a long flight to a more mild place to winter, only to repeat the flight in the spring. Whether the robin is so logical in his reasoning is doubtful.

Probably the presence of robins upon the rim of the Canyon during the wintertime has been largely fostered by the advent of white men into this area. Perhaps the greatest inducement that causes him to deter from his southern migration is the abundance of breadcrumbs and scraps quite appeasing to the gastronomical bliss of robin red-breast.

It is now against park policy to feed any wildlife in the park, including birds, for a number of reasons. In addition to the problems of dependence and interference with migration, feeding trays may spread respiratory and other diseases among birds.

When sufficient food is put in convenient places, such as provided by the hotels and residents of the park, it serves to induce the robins to become permanent residents.

CROSSBILL

Mrs. Glen E. Sturdevant
September, 1927.

DULL CARE SELDOM KNOCKS at the door of the naturalist's wife. Each day brings forth its share of excitement, for she never can tell what animal, plant, insect, or bird is to occupy some place in her household obligations. My guests vary from burrowing spiders, camouflaging stick bugs, hairy tarantulas, and scorpions, to desert ferns and plants, brilliant colored lizards, birds, rodents, and small animals. It never pays to be curious in a naturalist's home either, for there is no guessing what may be concealed in any shape or form of receptacle.

My latest occupant, crossbill, is perhaps one of the safest and most interesting guests I have harbored. We found him, broken-winged, near one of the numerous rain tanks in our park. I placed the little creature in a paper shopping bag, but it wasn't long before I found that. . . . He had readily cut a hole in the bag and effected his escape. . . . I decided to engage him in the popcorn popper, which served my purpose excellently.

It was with as much reluctance as pity and tenderness that I took this curious charge upon myself. Most of my experiences with wild birds have been sad ones. Refusing to eat and drink and expressing terror and confusion at any service tendered, they usually pine away and die. . . .

I was afraid that this little bird would follow the same course as my other wild birds. It was by accident that I received my delightful surprise. We had been out picking pinyon nuts in the morning, and just out of curiosity I placed a small pan of the fresh nuts in the crossbill's box . . . he partook of this new treat in an unrestrained measure of enjoyment.

After a week's time I allowed my little pinyon eater free range of the house. Every time he became hungry he would hop back to the little pan in which the nuts were placed, and every evening we were down on all fours looking for him to put him to bed. . . .

In a week or so the little wing may be fit for use again, but until the wings are a little stronger Mr. Crossbill must stay a little longer. . . .

OBSERVATION

P.P. Patraw, Assistant Superintendent
March, 1931.

ONE SATURDAY, FEBRUARY 7, I WITNESSED a short battle between a raven and a hawk. I was walking on the Bright Angel Trail about six hundred feet below the South Rim, when I heard a raven's raucous voice more noisesome even than usual. Rounding a short point, I saw ahead of me a raven and a hawk circling in the air. The raven would repeatedly gain the vantage point at the rear of and above the hawk, and then dive after the hawk. The hawk seemed easily to elude his pursuer after no more than momentary contact, and apparently without injury. After a half-dozen attacks, the raven tired and circled wider; the hawk began to climb on an air current without any movement of wing, the raven in pursuit. In a few spirals, the hawk gained the level of the rim and was soon only a moving speck against the gray winter sky, the raven still in pursuit but constantly losing "ground."

I was reminded of the air fights I had seen during the war, but the apparent unconcern of the hawk for his adversary made this battle much less interesting.

BIRD MIGRATION DATES

Edwin D. McKee, Park Naturalist
June, 1932.

IN A STUDY OF THE BIRDS of any region, it is always of interest and importance to record the dates of arrival and departure of various species that appear as visitants during migration. True, these data do not have particular significance unless kept over a period of years, however, it is felt that "Nature Notes" is the logical place to record such annual records as they are obtained, so that in the course of time any interested student of birds may have access to the material for the preparation of generalizations or for other reference.

April 17: Northern Pine Siskin, Grand Canyon Village.
April 30: Audubon's Warbler, Grand Canyon Village.
May 9: Grace's Warbler, Yavapai Road.
May 9: Greenbacked Goldfinch, Mohave Point.
May 10: Rocky Mountain Grosbeak, Yaki Point.

JUNCO VISITS BOTH RIMS

Edwin D. McKee, Park Naturalist
June, 1933.

ON DECEMBER 16, 1932, a red-backed junco was officially given the number of H-72850 at the Grand Canyon Birdbanding Station C, which is located at the McHenry residence on the South Rim. Four months later, April 20, 1933, Junco H-72850 appeared on the opposite rim of Grand Canyon, where it obligingly went into a trap operated by Ranger Hamilton at Substation E, on Bright Angel Point. This is important as the first definite cross-canyon bird record, and is suggestive of the many interesting data which may be expected as a result of continued banding in the park.

OBSERVATIONS

March, 1932.

WESTERN BELTED KINGFISHERS, of which we have comparatively few previous records from the Canyon, were numerous along Bright Angel Creek all winter.

June, 1929.

A BEAUTIFUL LITTLE PYGMY NUTHATCH NEST was observed upon this date in a juniper just in front of the Hopi House, South Rim. Voices of the inmates were noted.

July, 1928.

RANGER GEO. M. NILES, stationed at the Navahopi Ranger Station near Desert View, sighted four adult dusky grouse at Lipan Point during the month. Although grouse are very common on the North Rim, this is the first record of their occurrence on this rim of the Grand Canyon. . . . Ranger Niles is familiar with this species of grouse, and his observations are undoubtedly correct.

August, 1930.

PRAIRIE FALCONS HAVE BEEN SEEN and heard almost daily during August below Yavapai and Yaki Points in the Canyon. A pair of these marauders have been reported on several occasions as being dangerously near the birdfeeding stations at Grand Canyon Village.

October 1928.

THE MAJESTIC AMERICAN BALD EAGLE was sighted recently in the Grand Canyon. Peering over a ledge way down in the narrow, lonely depths of Hance Canyon, I was thrilled with a view of this noble bird, with head and tail of white. At a distance of scarcely a hundred yards, it splashed about in an isolated pool at the top of the Redwall. Although golden eagles have been noted upon numerous occasions, this is the first definite record that we have of our national bird in Grand Canyon.

Bald eagles seldom used to stop in their northward migrations over the Grand Canyon. However in the 1980s, these enormous birds discovered trout spawning in Nankoweap Creek, a tributary of the Colorado River that is about sixty-five miles downstream of Glen Canyon Dam. Two dozen or more bald eagles now spend about a week each spring feasting on the spawning trout. Biologists believe that this opportunity may become critical to the western population of bald eagles as other food sources dwindle. It appears that human interference with the river's natural system (planting fish eggs and constructing the dam) may be lessening some problems bald eagles face because of human interference elsewhere.

October, 1930.

HUMMINGBIRDS, notably broadtailed and rufous, are common on North and South Rims when hollyhocks, or such red trumpets as the gilias and scarlet buglers, are in bloom. A little way below Yaki Point on the Kaibab Trail, the scarlet buglers are so abundant that a whole flock of these shrilly, buzzing mites are ever on hand.

December, 1931.

DURING THE FOUR DAYS spent along Bright Angel Creek between November 17 and 21, I found the ashy ruby-crowned kinglets to be extremely numerous. Both individuals and small flocks were seen in the trees and shrubs all along the stream course.

SOME WILDLIFE OBSERVATIONS

Russell Grater, Ranger Naturalist
July, 1934.

A WESTERN CHIPPING SPARROW AND HIS MATE were endeavoring to fill the stomachs of their ever-hungry nestful of youngsters one recent, sunshiny morning, May 21, when there came a rude interruption in the form of a Gila chipmunk. Whatever his objective might have been in wanting to climb the tree containing the Sparrow family, it was never achieved! Instantly, the male chipping sparrow was metamorphosed from a quiet, timid, little creature into a raging, shrieking mass of angry feathers and snapping eyes. For a moment, the chipmunk endeavored to offer some opposition, but he was hopelessly outclassed and was forced to make a very inglorious retreat, leaving the victorious chipping sparrow in control of the situation.

This goes to prove that sufficient courage, if applied in the right manner, can overcome some exceedingly large obstacles.

American Bald Eagle

CHAPTER VII
Mammals

CHAMPION BARKER

Glen E. Sturdevant, Park Naturalist
March, 1928.

WHAT ANIMAL IS THE CHAMPION barker? Perhaps in answering, one might wish to consider quality and volume. If these were considered negligible factors, the Gila chipmunk would probably be a strong favorite to win first honors.

Recently, one posted himself on a dead branch outside of the door, and started to bark very rapidly. Until the source of disturbance was located, one might have been led to believe, from the penetrating character of the monotonous tones, that they came from a young bird. As time dragged on and the chipmunk failed to ease up in his calls, I was curious to know how many he emitted per minute. During three, separated minutes, his barks numbered 172, 146, and 162, respectively. As he remained in his position a little more than one-half hour and there was no noticeable change in barks, he must have barked in the neighborhood of 5,800 times in thirty minutes. Each bark was accompanied by a twitch of the tail.

OBSERVATION

July, 1933.

IN THE EARLY PART of last fall, a group of Gila chipmunks decided that the interior of the women's dormitory on the South Rim of the Grand Canyon afforded excellent places for nestbuilding. In the back porch, they found a bag of pinyon nuts and immediately went to work, explored the house for hiding places, and were successful.

The girls were, at first, mystified to find the coffee pot half full of nuts, little depressions in the bedding filled with nuts, nuts hidden in the floor mop, and even the shoes in the closet were not spared.

POCKET MICE

Edwin D. McKee, Park Naturalist
April, 1931.

DOWN ON THE TONTO PLATFORM of Grand Canyon may be seen many of the short, simple burrows made by a species of pocket mouse. These holes, which are about one inch in diameter, are usually placed in the loose, sandy soil at the base of bushes or shrubs. In the daytime, they are often plugged with soil.

Of the mammals to which the name mouse has been applied, there have been thirteen species recorded from the Grand Canyon. The grasshopper mouse, the harvest mouse, the meadow mouse, and the six varieties of white-footed mouse are all in the same family, while the pocket mouse is in another. The house mouse—so disliked by most people—belongs to still a different family. Fortunately, there are no records of his presence at Grand Canyon.

Probably the only close resemblance that the pocket mouse bears to the other mice is in size. He is a small rodent with a very long tail, large hind feet, and poorly developed claws on the forefeet. He has external, fur-lined cheek pockets, much like those of the pocket gopher. . . .

The general knowledge of pocket mice is comparatively limited, both because of their small size and because, being entirely nocturnal, they are seldom seen. Their food consists principally of seeds, which they eat by using their front feet as hands. As already mentioned, their enlarged hind feet enable them to bound along much like a kangaroo—their tail acting as stabilizer. They are also known to crawl or creep along. Breeding is in late spring. Altogether, this little rodent is one of the most interesting, yet least known mammals found within the boundaries of the Grand Canyon National Park.

BUTTON, BUTTON, WHO HAS THE BUTTON?

September, 1926.

WINESS IS STATIONED at the Bright Angel Ranger Station on the North Rim of the Grand Canyon. He enjoys the parties held at the Wylie Way summer camp, a short distance from the ranger station, equally as well as the people at the camp rejoice at the heartrending tales sung to the accompaniment of his wonderful guitar. Assured of his guitar being in good tune, Winess was putting on his dress suit for the occasion, when lo! to his amazement he noticed a lack of buttons. All of the buttons had been clipped from his coat. Accusation of his roommate as an impractical joker availed him naught, for his roommate was in turn surprised to see several buttons missing from his own clothes. Slowly it dawned on him, from his earlier experiences in Yellowstone, that the work was probably that of a pack or trade rat. Since buttons are not appetizing food even for rats, Winess put forth a diligent search for the objects in question. He was baffled completely until he at last located the buttons, as well as small sticks and other objects, in a bulging pocket of the coat.

With a vow of no more roommates occupying his quarters unbeknown to him, Winess stopped up the rathole, sewed on the buttons, and directed his steps toward the camp.

A CURIOUS COLLECTION

Russell Grater, Ranger Naturalist
October, 1934.

NEAR THE MUSEUM, a San Francisco Mountain woodrat has painstakingly built himself a home. An investigation of his dwelling revealed the astonishing fact that, in addition to dirt and sticks, it contained:

1 piece of gauze.
3 blue-headed pins from the museum.
3 grains of corn, Hopi variety.
2 burnt matches.
3 different shades of thread.
1 piece of tire tape.
A quantity of electric light wiring.
2 types of beans (evidently a part of the archaeological display in the museum).
1 piece of tinfoil.
1 button.
1 piece of isinglass.
1 cigar wrapper.
1 piece of cellophane.
1 part of a comic strip of newspaper.

1 piece of cloth.
1 small paper box.
1 length of lantern slide binding tape.
A few pinyon nuts.
A quantity of juniper berries.

KAIBAB SQUIRREL; ABERT SQUIRREL

Glen E. Sturdevant, Park Naturalist
March, 1926.

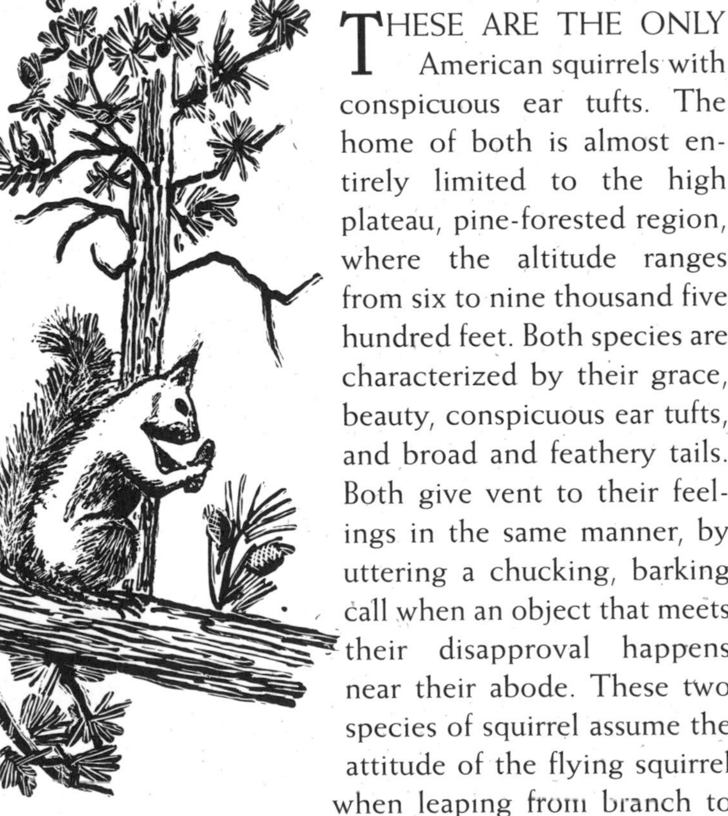

KAIBAB SQUIRREL

THESE ARE THE ONLY American squirrels with conspicuous ear tufts. The home of both is almost entirely limited to the high plateau, pine-forested region, where the altitude ranges from six to nine thousand five hundred feet. Both species are characterized by their grace, beauty, conspicuous ear tufts, and broad and feathery tails. Both give vent to their feelings in the same manner, by uttering a chucking, barking call when an object that meets their disapproval happens near their abode. These two species of squirrel assume the attitude of the flying squirrel when leaping from branch to branch. They spread out their limbs and tail to the utmost, particularly when they descend from a high branch to the ground. During a storm, the squirrel seeks his nest for shelter, where he remains until the inclement weather is over. . . .

Originally considered to be of the same species, the powerful factor of isolation has brought about radical changes in the marking of the two species. The Abert squirrel is characterized by his gray tail, the downy white markings on the underparts, the broad, reddish-brown stripe along his back, and his grey sides. The Kaibab squirrel, whose environment is entirely limited to an island-like, pine-forested area on the North Rim of the Grand Canyon, is even more beautiful than his cousin. His tail is a feathery white, with the underparts appearing almost solid black.

OBSERVATIONS

April, 1932.

THE YOUNG OF SEVERAL MAMMALS have already made their appearance around Grand Canyon Village this spring. Immature Abert squirrels were first reported on March 25th, and baby chipmunks on April 12th.

July, 1934.

A FEMALE ABERT SQUIRREL was seen one morning in early May with a mouthful of strips of juniper bark and dry pine needles. . . . While I watched, she carefully pushed the needles and juniper bark into the top of her nest and patted them in place. . . .

The explanation for this reconstruction work appeared obvious. Although the nest had been skillfully built a month or more previously, it had never been tested in rain. Indeed, the dry spell of this past spring probably helped materially in developing lines of weakness, which the heavy rains of the previous night had exposed.

DINING SOLITAIRE

Earl W. Count, Ranger Naturalist
August, 1930.

VISITORS WHO COME TO THE SOUTH RIM frequently encounter the little rock squirrel, and are distinctly reminded of the common gray squirrel found in various forms over most of the United States. But the rock squirrel hugs the ground, and leaves it only occasionally. He is frequently to be seen along the rim of the Canyon. . . .

Traveling down the brink one day, I met a little rock squirrel sprawled over a serviceberry bush, pulling twigs towards him from all sides and nipping off the fruits. Gradually, his cheeks below his ears swelled out, giving him the ridiculous appearance of a case of mumps. He did not mind me; he clambered down, passed me within a few inches, then disappeared down the Canyon. Farther on, I at last came upon him again, perched on the brink of a remote little cave in the limestone where he could command a soul-filling view of the Canyon depths. One berry after another he worked forward from his cheeks, held it in his paws, chewed out the seeds with that squirrel chatter of the jaws, then with some quick, glancing pats of one paw against the other, such as you would use to slap dust or grime from your hands, or a sudden, babyish toss of those paws, he sent the hulls of the fruit fluttering Canyonward.

This charming observation is a reminder that visitors may enjoy watching the squirrels at Grand Canyon without feeding them the human foods—too rich in fat, too salty or sweet, too processed—that make them unhealthy and dependent. Rock squirrels are far better off (and more fun to watch) clambering over serviceberry bushes in pursuit of a *wholesome* mouthful.

NOTES ON PORCUPINES OF THE GRAND CANYON REGION

Charles M. Bogert, Ranger Naturalist
April, 1933.

BECAUSE OF THE NOCTURNAL propensities of the porcupine, few people become acquainted with this, the second largest of the present-day rodents in North America. Nevertheless, in the forests of both the Kaibab and Coconino Plateaus, porcupines are quite abundant. . . .

Porcupines in this region normally spend the day in treetops, selecting a position where foliage obscures them from the ground. . . .

While Grand Canyon is probably a fairly effective barrier for this species, porcupines are not confined entirely to forested Transition Zone habitats but seem occasionally to range well down into the Upper Sonoran Zone. Evidences of their food-getting activities are prominent along both rims of Grand Canyon, and on the South Rim at least, the pinyon pine is most often selected. Judging by the chips left, the outer layer of dead bark is removed and only the sap-filled, growing, cambium layer is eaten. While scars left by this gnawing sometimes cover extensive areas (as much as a square foot in a single patch), never has the writer observed a tree that has been completely "ringed."

Young individuals liberated after a few hours of captivity, during which they had become quite tame, would amble off into the brush, pausing to nibble the green seeds from the desert mallow. Sitting on the hind limbs with the tail as a "prop," the four-fingered hands in front would be used in bringing the stems to the mouth and with the incisors the foliage and buds would be stripped off, with intermissions for chewing and swallowing. A young captive specimen devoured cantaloupe rinds (not too readily) and groaned most of the following day, exhibiting evident signs of discomfiture.

OBSERVATION

May, 1930.

ON THE EVENING OF MAY 15TH, a porcupine was seen ascending the Bright Angel Trail about a hundred feet below the rim. He seemed very much out of place, but did not appear to be half so tired as most of the tourist hikers.

THE SONORA BEAVER

Chester R. Markley, Park Ranger
June, 1931.

THE CASUAL MOTORIST to the Grand Canyon usually gives little attention to the emblem on the sticker which is placed on the windshield of his car. There are others, however, who ask the name of the animal framed in the Canyon setting. Some recognize it as the beaver, and are surprised to hear that he lives within the Canyon walls.

The beaver has been written about since the early days of our history; he was a goal that led pioneers to explore the far reaches of the land. His life habits—engineering skill in particular—are known to every schoolboy, but how many people have seen him in his natural state?

. . . The Colorado River—muddy, swift, and treacherous, with deep eddies and whirlpools—makes it perhaps the most dangerous river in our country to navigate, yet the beaver used this fearful river as his highway of travel. . . .

While passing within the Canyon walls, the beaver encountered many streams of clear, cold water, the objects of his trips. Wherever permanent water flowed through the lower reaches of the Canyon, he found a luxuriant growth of cottonwood and willow, trees for which he was endlessly searching. He worked his way up the roaring streams, many of which had a fall of three thousand feet in seven to ten miles. Often his progress was suddenly interrupted by waterfalls which dropped over precipitous cliffs that he could not scale. Disappointed, he would return to the Colorado and swim up the mouth of the next stream, and where the ascent was possible, find a new home, a home that was as strange as the muddy Colorado. . . .

Visitors often ask about the wire cages around the cottonwoods at Phantom Ranch. The wire is intended to "beaver-proof" the trees.

Often during the low water stages of the stream, he may construct a dam and start work on his lodge, but eventually the spring freshets or stormwaters of midsummer will destroy in a single night the results of many months of labor. Often under such adverse conditions, the beaver will build a den in the bank of the stream with an underwater entrance usually on the leeward side of a huge rock projecting out into a pool, using the surface of the rock as a sidewall of the burrow leading to the den. Here again, the beaver meets the inevitable, for sand and gravel soils are poor materials in which to burrow, with the result that his burrow caves in. With sorrow and disappointment in his heart, the beaver roams from the mouth of the streams to their source, or as far as progress is possible. . . .

Only very rarely do we find a sly old beaver who has adapted himself or his ideas of engineering to meet local conditions. In occasional places, a beaver has constructed a combination lodge and bank den with one entrance underwater, or with an exit above the water surface as well as below it.

THE RACCOON OF HAVASUPAI

Chester R. Markley, Park Ranger
March, 1931.

HERE LIVES the pallid raccoon. When and how he came to be in Havasu Canyon is an unsolved puzzle. The closest neighbor of this species is reported along the Colorado River near Needles, over two hundred miles away. Lacking an important article of diet—fish—the little animal has turned to the natural food of fish that abounds along Cataract Creek: insects and insect larvae. . . . Evidence indicates that during the summer and early fall, his diet includes wild grapes, berries, and corn from the outlying fields. In the spring and summer, small birds and eggs undoubtedly are taken and devoured by the 'coons during their nightly raids along the banks of the stream. . . .

During the month of February, I planted Cataract Creek with rainbow fry, which were strong and healthy five days after planting. If conditions remain favorable, the raccoons may in the future acquire that item of their diet which has been lacking: fish.

RINGTAILED CATS

Mrs. Glen E. Sturdevant
October, 1928.

A COUPLE OF MONTHS AGO, two half-grown ringtailed cats were caught in the dining room at Phantom Ranch. They were boxed and sent by muleback as a donation for the park museum. Since caged or leashed wild animals are not approved of in national park museums, the task of taming these two accessories had to be undertaken.

Mr. and Mrs. Brooks (Chief Ranger and wife) volunteered to undertake this interesting work. . . . They donated the whole back porch to the "cats," leaving them free to roam around as they wished . . . until a crack in the porch door allowed their wards to take "French leave." All was not lost, however, by their departure, for during their brief sojourn many interesting habits were observed. . . .

The cats were not finical, as their appetites soon proved. Although they are omnivorous, they decidedly favored a meat diet. Raw meat was preferred to cooked meat, and mice to any meat obtained at the market. Fish was not liked at all. The old barn cat, who is quite a mouser, unbeknown to herself furnished her rivals with two mice each day. After catching the mice, the old cat would take them to Mrs. Brooks, who in turn would give them to the ringtails. . . . But the most delectable dish of all to them seemed to be grapes. It was for these that they would venture forth from their various and sundry hiding places (woodboxes, refrigerator, etc.), creeping up hesitatingly and then with a graceful movement of their heads, snatch them prettily to eat in privacy. The other two articles of diet which they seemed to enjoy were eggs and milk. . . .

Ringtailed Cat

During the day, the cats slept one coiled on top the other

until they were hardly discernible from each other. Their repose was easily broken, however, sudden noises rousing them enough to show ugly claws and slashing teeth.

A rare treat was in store for those who could see them in the late evening. They frolicked and boxed and cavorted around like kittens, climbing all over the porch. . . . It was their greatest delight to push things off and knock every available hanging object down. . . . Nothing new ever came to the back porch which they did not examine, not even a fresh supply of kindling wood. After a short time, they even dared to nose Mr. and Mrs. Brooks, for whom they gradually lost fear.

The name "ringtailed cat" is scarcely fitting for these animals; for although they are ring-tailed, they are not cats but rather belong to the raccoon family. The ringtailed cat is one of the most interesting animals, in that so many different animal characteristics are present in this one. With a weasel-like body, fox-like face, cat-like feet, and raccoon-like tail, he appears as the final product of a four-animal melting pot.

THE COMMON SKUNK

Glen E. Sturdevant, Park Naturalist
November, 1926.

LIMITED ENTIRELY TO NORTH AMERICA, the common skunk (*Mephitis mephitis*), with a thorough knowledge of the efficacy of his own peculiar means of defense, has held his own against the inroads of civilization upon his natural domain.

Resembling the badger to some extent, in general appearance and the lengthened claws of the forefeet, the skunk is found to differ decidedly from the weasel family (*Mustelidae*), to which it belongs. . . . The skunk is not built for speed. His ponderous body appears to weigh heavily on the small feet. In fact "haste" does not appear in his dictionary, as is evidenced by his slow movements even when cornered. Why should he hurry? Apparently cognizant of knowing no master, the skunk pursues his desultory course in a leisurely manner. . . .

The skunk presents a curious combination of industry and indolence. When making his nocturnal prowls for food, he spares no effort to provide himself with the necessities of life. Patiently he works, turning over innumerable small rocks to see if some cricket or other edible insect is not hidden beneath. . . .

Although loathing to dig his own hole, Mr. Skunk sees apparently no reason why he should go without one. He is quite adept at appropriating some burrowing animal's quarters, or making his home under some residence. When the home is once selected, the skunk is not sloven in making it comfortable. Regardless of the size of the apartment, dry leaves and grass are carried in until the home is made small enough to meet the needs of the one or more individuals occupying it.

The skunk is a gregarious being. Up to seventeen members have been known to occupy a single den. . . .

The mating season takes place early in March. The latter part of April or the forepart of May marks an important advent in the home life of the prolific skunk. At this time, four to ten of the future odoriferous members appear in the nest.

The aversion of the skunk to building his own home at the Grand Canyon has caused mutual alarm and consternation on the part of the canyon residents and manager of the Bright Angel cottages. This confiscation by the skunk of the unused space beneath the floor has not been welcomed. Although the presence of skunks marks an absence of mice, the lesser of two evils is preferable.

OBSERVATION

May, 1929.

THE LITTLE SPOTTED SKUNKS (*Spilogale gracilis*) are reported as numerous this summer at Indian Gardens.

THE BADGER AND ITS ENVIRONMENT

Chester R. Markley, Park Ranger
January, 1931.

ON THE SOUTH RIM OF THE CANYON, where there is an intermingling of the Upper Sonoran and Transition Life Zones, lives the wolverine of the south, known as the badger. . . . It is an animal easily recognized by his robust body and short legs, the feet of which are armed with long, strong claws. These claws are his weapons and means of obtaining a livelihood, with which he digs up his prey with the tenacity of the wolverine. His courage and strength are to be feared by any animal his size. . . .

The washes and draws through the yellow pine and pinyon-juniper type forests are his home; usually in or near a prairie dog town, and occasionally in any clearing in the pinyon-juniper forest where he has located the homes of the ground squirrel, rock squirrel, chipmunk, pocket gopher, or any small member of the rodent family.

OBSERVATION

March, 1933.

MOUNTAIN WEASEL—These large weasels, *Mustila frenata arizonensis*, range from central Arizona to Oregon. Although known to occur on both sides of Grand Canyon, they are seldom found on the South Rim. Of much interest, therefore, was the discovery of one, dead, in the barn of the Fred Harvey Company.

LADY HECATE

Barbara Hastings
June, 1929.

LADY HECATE WAS MY PET for several days at Phantom Ranch during May. She was one of the small red bats—*Myotis californicus*—which can be seen in great numbers circling and swooping in Bright Angel Canyon just at dusk. . . .

I kept Lady Hecate for two days and let her go the third night. She became too insistent for food. By the third night she had become so tame that I could not go in my cabin that she did not light on my sleeves or shoulder and crawl to my hand to be fed. She drank drops of water from my fingertips and then licked my fingers. I fed her at least six large millers [moths] the third night. She would hang calmly upside down on the screen and chew them. I could hear her little teeth cracking. Generally she was most fastidious and was careful not to eat the wings of the moths. They would flutter to the floor after the last chew.

A BITTER STRUGGLE

Edwin D. McKee, Park Naturalist
October, 1932.

THERE WAS A PRONOUNCED SOUND of fluttering nearby. Low over the water of the mudtank where I stood fishing flew a large bat with long, slender wings. Its size and proportions were such that they immediately commanded my attention. They formed a marked contrast with those of the two best known bats of the region, the little pallid bat and the canyon bat.

Even while I watched this winged mammal and wondered concerning its identity, a strange thing occurred. Coming from the opposite end of the tank, another and similar bat approached. With rapid stroke of wings the two flew straight to-

PALLID BAT

ward each other, and for no apparent reason crashed in mid-air. For a brief moment they whirled about, flapped their wings furiously, uttered strange, squeaking sounds, and then dropped like two bolts. In the dim twilight, one of the bats disappeared from sight but the other was plainly visible as it slowly swam toward shore, using both wings in a type of breaststroke. By running along the water's edge, I was able to reach and easily catch this one before it crawled up on the land. Also, to my great surprise, I found the other bat lying nearby on a flat rock—apparently stunned. Thus, a double capture was accomplished.

After only a brief moment, both bats seemed to revive, and both regained their fighting spirits simultaneously. The one which had just previously been swimming grabbed the other by the wing with a "bull dog" grip. The other uttered weird noises and vainly attempted to retaliate. Indeed, considerable force was necessary to separate the animals, and individual containers were required for peace. . . .

Upon examination, the bats proved to be of a variety known as the pallid brown bat.

A NEAR TRAGEDY

March, 1928.

ASSISTANT SUPERINTENDENT P.P. PATRAW was a recent witness to one of the many life battles that take place daily in the great outdoors. As usual, the strong was preying upon the weak, but both participants escaped with their lives. . . . Near the road, he saw a "rock" having an outline of a very large hawk. As he called attention to the fact, the "rock" started to flap its wings and became a hawk in reality. The hawk experienced difficulty in rising. He could be seen skimming the earth in a series of ups and downs, with an Arizona cottontail dangling in his talons. At last the cottontail broke loose, and bounded to cover in the sagebrush while the hawk circled the area for his intended prey.

KAIBAB DEER . . . ON SOUTH RIM

E.T. Scoyen, Chief Ranger
September, 1926.

PERHAPS THE MOST INTERESTING AND DRAMATIC event in connection with wildlife conservation in the United States is the famous Kaibab deer drive, which was attempted two years ago. The fact that the project was unique and that the means employed was to be based on an ancient Indian method gave the proceeding a spectacular aspect, and consequently a firm grip on the imagination of the public.

The drive was a failure. In spite of glowing statements of the ease by which ten thousand wild deer could be collected into one herd, forced over the rim of the Grand Canyon, and then herded across the great gorge to the rim on the other side, the attempt ended almost before it started. Not a single deer even saw the trail leading into the canyon, and at the agreed delivery rate on the South Rim of one dollar per head, the gross receipts were zero. . . .

There were many reasons why the attempt failed. The most prominently mentioned are the lack of organization and the great storm which broke at a critical moment. These were probably contributory, but the fundamental one was the fact that Mr. Deer refused to be driven, and no collection of cowbells and whooping Indians was terrifying enough to make him leave his home range.

FLYING DEER

P.P. Patraw, Assistant Superintendent
October, 1929.

ON SUNDAY AFTERNOON, September 29, eight fawns from the famous Kaibab deer herd took an airplane ride over the Grand Canyon as guests of Scenic Airways, Incorporated. So far as known, this is the first time that deer have taken to wings and invaded the domain of the eagle. . . .

The question of the Kaibab deer herd outgrowing its limited range has long been disputed, but after careful study of conditions by government biological experts, it is now generally accepted that the herd is too large for the carrying capacity of the range, is eating itself gradually out of house and home, and must be reduced. The National Park Service favors trapping and exportation to effect as much as possible by this means the reduction of the herd and its annual increase, and attempts to encourage this by annually importing a few fawns to the South Rim. Fawns are trapped under permits issued by the U.S. Forest Service, which also arranges for their disposal. They are captured by the use of specially trained dogs, which run them down and hold them with forepaws until the hunters come up.

A UNIQUE COMBINATION

J.P. Brooks, Chief Ranger
March, 1930.

A SEMI-TAME BAND OF MULE DEER at Grand Canyon have adopted, or perhaps only accepted, two rabbits into their clan. It cannot be truthfully said that this comradeship was entirely sponsored by the deer, however, for it was rather a forced intrusion on the part of the rabbits. During the winter months, the latter were attracted to the deer feedyards

MULE DEER

by the hay and barley. At first, the rabbits were somewhat shy, and contented themselves solely with what food they could pick up on the ground. However, they soon adapted themselves to their new surroundings, becoming more chummy with the deer from day to day, feeding alongside them at the grain troughs, and nibbling from the same stalks of hay . . . They made up to the deer in many ways, bedded down alongside and amongst them, nestled close to them and climbed on their backs, and often standing on their hind legs, nosed the faces of the deer. . . . The fawns . . . would nose, even lick the rabbits with apparent signs of friendliness and affection.

When the deer left the feedyards at sundown on their nightly rambles through the adjacent forest, the rabbits accompanied them and returned with the band at daylight. The deer, apparently accepting the company, would lift their feet and carefully place them so as not to strike the rabbits jumping in and out under them.

BUCKS GROW BOLD

Barbara Hastings McKee
February, 1934.

THAT THE BUCK MULE DEER at Grand Canyon are very zealous in guarding their mates was amply demonstrated last November. As the rutting season advanced, these bucks developed as usual into powerful beasts with swollen necks and towering antlers. . . . Because of constant association throughout the year with the people of Grand Canyon Village, these mule deer even when their very nature changes do not fear human beings, so it is the better part of valor for the people to avoid all lovesick bucks. . . .

Feeding of deer ended in the 1930s, when the animals became a nuisance. The park no longer feeds any wildlife, because the philosophy of the National Park Service is to maintain Grand Canyon in as natural a state as possible. Biologists have determined that deer are better nourished by browsing on a variety of shrubs, trees, grasses, sedges, and mushrooms than by consuming just

Ernest Ensor, trail caretaker at Indian Gardens in the Canyon, early one morning in November went out to the deer and antelope feeding grounds and started to put hay into the racks. Without warning a huge buck, which had been standing a short distance away, leaped over the feeding trough and, catching Mr. Ensor by the arm and leg with its antlers, dragged him some thirty feet into the underbrush. The sleeve of Mr. Ensor's leather jacket and his shirt sleeve were torn and his arm was cut. Fortunately the other antler merely tore his trousers and did not penetrate to the skin.

hay and barley. Deer are also migratory animals, and need to move about rather than linger near feedyards. Mule deer migrate to lower elevations in the fall in search of browse and so that rutting males can distance themselves from one another. In early spring, does seek solitude to give birth. However, some visitors still insist upon feeding the deer, even stopping in the middle of the road to hold snacks out to them through the windows of their cars! The resulting "deer-jams" can cause auto accidents, and luring deer onto the asphalt is *very* hazardous for the deer.

DEER ANTLERS

Clyde C. Searl, Ranger Naturalist
October, 1930.

IF ONE WANTED TO ARGUE THE POINT, deer do not really lose their horns, inasmuch as they do not have horns to begin with. True horns are found in oxen, sheep, and antelope. The horns of deer, being solid, are technically called antlers.

Antlers are simply protuberances of the frontal skull bone. While growing, the outgrowths are covered with sensitive, vascular, hairy skin, commonly called velvet. The blood supply to the antler stops as soon as the growth is completed. When the blood supply ceases, the skin dies and peels off, leaving the bone bare, and in the later winter the bones, by a process of absorption near the base, become detached from the skull and are dropped. This process is repeated every year; the new antlers budding out on the stumps left by the shedding of the old ones.

ANTLERS AS AN AGE INDICATOR OF DEER

October, 1928.

THAT ONE CANNOT BE SURE OF THE AGE of a deer from the number of points on the antlers is evidenced by the marked variation of horns worn by three tame bucks of approximately the same age at Grand Canyon National Park.

All three bucks were caught shortly after birth, in the early summer of 1927. At the present time, all are entering their second winter—their summer red coats having been replaced with gray winter coats and their horns having been polished of the velvet indicating the full growth for the first season. . . .

The age criteria of a single spike for each antler, however, is present on only one buck. The antlers as an age indicator would hardly work in the case of the other two. For not knowing the age, one might easily believe they had entered upon their third or fourth winter. One buck has three points and eye guard on one antler and three points on the other antler. The third buck possesses a beautiful set of antlers, with three points and a well-developed eye guard on each horn.

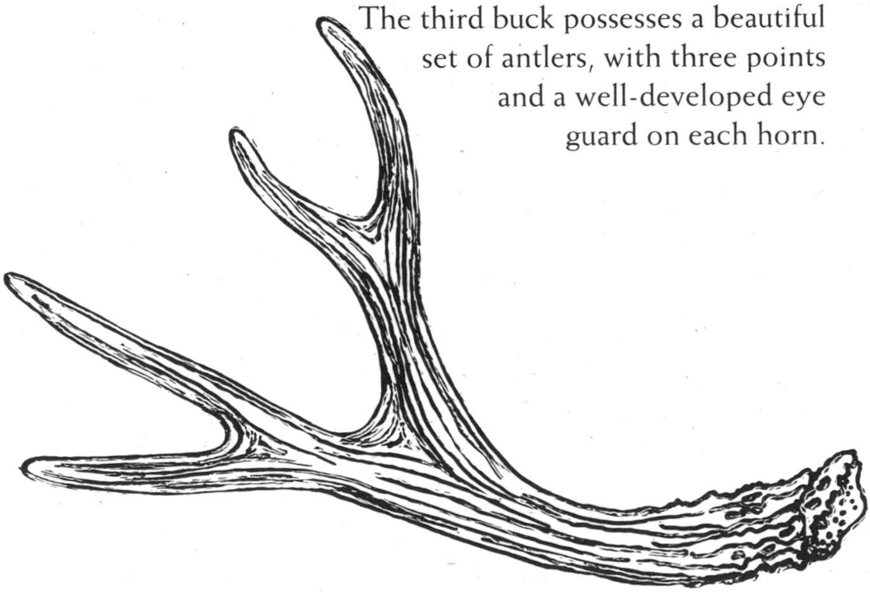

OBSERVATIONS

January, 1934.

ON SEVERAL OCCASIONS during the last month, some of the C.C.C. boys stationed in the bottom of the Canyon near Phantom Ranch have reported being eyewitnesses to deer swimming the Colorado River. On one of these occasions, they were surprised at the manner by which a doe and her two fawns estimated the flow of the stream so that with the speed of the current and their swimming, they were able to land on the opposite side at the only possible place from which they could have climbed out of the water.

HERMIT STEER OF THE CANYON

May, 1928.

A RECENT VISIT to Phantom and Haunted Canyons on the north side of the Colorado River resulted in the discovery of an aged steer leading a detached life in this isolated region.

In 1916, when the Grand Canyon was a national monument supervised by the Forest Service, a permit to graze cattle on the Tonto Plateau was given to Scott Dunham of Fredonia, Arizona. Dunham brought his stock down Bright Angel Canyon, and headed them out on the plateau to Haunted and Phantom Canyons. At this place, Mr. Dunham established a camp under a huge cliff. If present conditions are indicative of the past, the steers found a bountiful supply of grass in the two canyons.

Upon creation of the Grand Canyon as a national park, the steers were driven out of the Canyon to market. One steer was missing. Some who were acquainted with conditions believed that the steer had perished, while others maintained that he still lived.

While visiting the region in April, unmistakable evidence was found of a steer that left extra large tracks. The tracks were followed up the stream in Phantom Canyon to a dense growth of cottonwoods. Failure to find tracks above the thicket suggested that he had headed back down the Canyon.

Such was found to be the case on the return journey, for the tracks indicated that the animal had eluded us while in the thicket, and returned down Phantom and up Haunted Canyon.

Although the age of the steer is not definitely known, he is believed to be from twelve to fifteen years old.

WILD BURROS OF THE GRAND CANYON

P.P. Patraw, Assistant Superintendent
May, 1930.

THE BANDS OF WILD BURROS making their homes on the Tonto Platform and up side canyons of the Grand Canyon developed from the animals lost or abandoned by prospectors many years ago. While conditions were far from favorable for existence, the burros demonstrated their hardihood and adaptability by prolific reproduction, until they overpopulated the range and had practically denuded the plateau of all vegetation save burrobush. Even cactus, with its protective bristling barbs and swords, was not proof against the demand of the burro for food, and was uprooted and eaten.

Classing the burro as an undesirable tenant, because he did not belong to the Canyon originally in Nature's scheme and was destroying the range properly belonging to native forms of wildlife—particularly the mountain sheep and the antelope—the National Park Service began a campaign of extermination on the south side of the river seven years ago. . . .

On the sections which have been freed from burros for a

period of four or more years, the range has recovered to such an extent as to furnish good grazing. Mountain sheep, while still scarce, are seen more frequently; also more deer are ranging the plateau in the wintertime. Two years after the extermination program was put into effect, wildflowers appeared that had not been seen for many years.

Not all of the burros were eliminated during this campaign, and the few that survived multiplied. Studies in the 1970s showed that burros were again devastating the vegetation of Grand Canyon and fouling its springs, to the detriment of other wildlife. In 1981, after public outcry had defeated a Park Service plan to shoot the burros, the Fund for Animals removed the animals by helicopter and put them up for adoption.

STATUS OF THE DESERT BIGHORN IN GRAND CANYON NATIONAL PARK

Edwin D. McKee, Park Naturalist
July, 1934.

ONE INTERESTING NATIVE ANIMAL of the Grand Canyon whose numbers cannot be counted or estimated with even a fair degree of accuracy is the desert, or Nelson, bighorn mountain sheep. This animal, which is known to range through many parts of Grand Canyon yet is seldom seen, has such a peculiar nature that it has never been possible by ordinary methods to make estimates of its abundance worth recording. It is for this reason that the writer has attempted to gather together from sources considered reliable all records of bighorns seen in Grand Canyon during the past five years. . . .

Mountain sheep are of general and not uncommon distribution along the entire Grand Canyon south of the Colorado River. They are most numerous above the Redwall and below the rim. . . .

Judging from observations made along several of the trails leading into Grand Canyon from the South Rim, mountain sheep stay in a rather restricted area for long periods, ranging about locally in small bands or singly (possibly varying with the season). In brief, it is believed that the large band or bands seen so often around Hermit Basin and below remain in this immediate area from year to year, probably because of the abundance of springs in this vicinity. On the other hand, a smaller and distinct group of sheep stay near the Bright Angel Trail and a ewe, which can be recognized absolutely and which is very tame, has been seen in that area many times during the past few years.

MOUNTAIN SHEEP OBSERVED ON CANYON RIM

December, 1927.

THE WORKMEN CONSTRUCTING the Observation Station at Yavapai Point were recently treated to the unusual experience of seeing a large ram mountain sheep near the building.

Shortly after commencing work, the ram was again sighted about thirty yards away. In order to obtain a picture of the sheep, several of the workmen tried to force him onto a rock shelf below the rim. The ram evidently sensed their intention, for he turned and faced his tormentors with lowered head, and began pawing the earth. This caused the workmen to scatter, and gave the mountain sheep an opportunity to descend into the Canyon.

BIGHORN SHEEP

February, 1929.

A LARGE MOUNTAIN SHEEP RAM, seen in the neighborhood of Havasupai Point on the South Rim of the Canyon instead of down on the slopes below the Canyon rim, represents a new record of this animal living upon the rim. At first, this animal was wild and timid, but as he became accustomed to the daily presence of members of a surveying party in the vicinity, he would run short distances and stand and watch the men of the party for long periods of time.

December, 1932.

WHILE HIKING IN THE VICINITY of Indian Gardens on November 18th, 1932, I came upon four mountain sheep at the base of the Redwall formation. Two were ewes, one a lamb about one-third grown and the other a ram. Although Nelson bighorn sheep are known to inhabit many parts of the Grand Canyon area, sight records of them are sufficiently scarce to justify mention in every case.

AN EXPERIMENTAL REPAIR JOB

E.T. Scoyen, Chief Ranger
February, 1928.

SEVERAL YEARS AGO, the American Bison Association and other conservation organizations found growing evidence that the antelope was in danger of being added to our list of extinct native wildlife. Since that time, every effort has been made to prevent such a tragedy. . . .

In connection with this work, a very interesting experiment is now being conducted in the Grand Canyon National Park. The records of early explorers show that antelope once occurred in the park in great numbers, but when the park was created in 1919, there was not a single pronghorn to be found within its boundaries. The present experiment is an effort to repair the damage that has already been done by reintroducing these animals into this area in which they were completely killed off. . . .

About 3,100 feet below the rim, the Grand Canyon flattens out and forms a narrow shelf about an average of one-half mile in width; this is called the Tonto Plateau. . . . From certain angles, the location was ideal. The animals could not get away because the canyon walls shut them in, water was plentiful, and the area was free from large, predatory animals. The only problem related to forage conditions, as the hundreds of wild burros had practically destroyed the natural vegetation. . . .

AMERICAN PRONGHORN

Since the herd was introduced, we have suffered the loss of three does and two bucks. Counting the increase this year, there are now 10 animals in the herd, a net loss of two since they were introduced. This part of the problem causes but little concern, as we never doubted but that there would be some deaths.

In many ways, this is probably one of the most interesting little bands of animals to be found anywhere. They are as tame as any domestic animal. I have seen tourists try to photograph them, but they secure good pictures only by expending a considerable amount of patience. This is due not to the wildness of the animals, but to the difficulty in keeping far enough away. . . .

It is still too early to try and predict the final outcome of the experiment. Although these little animals are very close to our hearts, we must keep in mind the fact that the entire project is still in its experimental stage. At times during the year they look fine, and other times not so good. It is my opinion that if they weather the next year successfully, there is a very good chance that the experiment will be a success.

The pronghorn herd grew from nine to thirty animals, but died out after the Park Service stopped feeding them in 1936. There are no pronghorn on the Tonto Platform today.

. . . THE AMERICAN PRONGHORN

Ralph A. Redburn, Ranger Naturalist
November, 1931.

THE VISITOR, on seeing one of the pronghorns for the first time, probably associates it with some kind of deer. However, it does not belong to the deer family (*Cervidae*), neither is it a true antelope (*Bovidae*), but belongs to a family of its own (*Antilocapridae*), of one-pronged, deciduous-horned* animals. . . .

*After the breeding season, pronghorns shed the outer covering of their horns, exposing the permanent bony sheaths beneath.

OBSERVATIONS

July, 1932.

A TOTAL OF EIGHT KID PRONGHORN antelopes, from either four or five mothers, is reported from Indian Gardens this year.

May, 1934.

THREE NATIVE AMERICAN PRONGHORN ANTELOPE were seen at Buggeln Hill, South Rim, on April 12. They were very wild, and loped off through the sagebrush toward the Canyon rim.

A COYOTE TALE

Ralph A. Redburn, Ranger Naturalist
March, 1933.

THE COYOTE OF THE NORTH RIM REGION is usually seen in "park" areas, which are open plateau meadows in the forest. . . . In these areas, the coyote finds grasshoppers upon which to feed. Often last summer, as many as four coyotes were seen in the same meadow at the same time. . . .

On the other hand, not infrequently while traveling along the highways which lead through the forest to the rim of the Canyon, one could see coyotes sitting at the edge of the road. After passing such places many times, it became obvious why these animals had so located themselves. They had learned that they need not run after food any more. All that was necessary to obtain a meal was to wait by the highway for a car to run over a squirrel, chipmunk, mouse, or some other creature.

OBSERVATIONS

June, 1930.

MEMBERS OF THE CARNEGIE EXPEDITION to the little-known Nankoweap Canyon reported having seen many coyote tracks and heard the animals close by their camp. This is the first record that we have received of coyotes in the Canyon bottom.

November, 1933.

AN ARIZONA GRAY FOX WAS SEEN in the center of the road at a point between the main highway and Yavapai Observation Station, about 7:15 p.m. on October 7, 1933. He paused for a moment, blinded by the headlights of the car, and then slowly trotted off into the darkness on the east side of the road.

FOX HOLDS UP PARTY

June, 1927.

AN INTERESTING INCIDENT OCCURRED during Dr. John C. Merriam's recent visit to Grand Canyon National Park.

Dr. Merriam was in the lead on the return trip up the Yaki Point section of the Kaibab Trail. "Rastus," a park mule on which he was seated, gradually slowed up. . . . At last came a call from Dr. Merriam to "chase that fox up the trail so Rastus can continue." True enough, a grey fox with a mouse in his mouth was setting a very slow pace up the trail. The fears of Rastus seemed wholly relieved when the fox left the trail a short distance ahead.

A pair of foxes has been sighted a number of times in the same vicinity during the past few months, causing us to believe that their den was not a great distance away. That our supposition concerning the presence of the den was correct is evidenced by the report of the trail maintenance man seeing the pair with two half-grown pups only a few days ago.

BARE FACTS ABOUT BEAR TRACKS

George L. Collins, Park Ranger
June, 1931.

DURING THE PAST FEW YEARS, rumors have originated from time to time concerning the presence of bear along the South Rim of Grand Canyon. Records show that a few were seen years ago in the North Rim country, but on the South Rim until recently, our bear stories have all proved to be simply unsubstantiated tales or rumors. . . .

Our latest bear rumor started its rounds quite recently. We were, of course, all ears as the underlying story unfolded, which it did pretty much as follows:

Mr. Miles Polson, employee of Fred Harvey at Hermits Rest, . . . was returning home on the evening of June 15 from a trip into Grand Canyon Village. As he passed the old tram-house near Pima Point, he was very much surprised indeed to see a medium-sized bear charge across the road within the headlight range of his car.

Mr. Polson, being a man of excellent discretion, decided that it would not do to report such an occurrence without first making sure that he was absolutely right in his classification of the animal, though both he and Mrs. Polson, who was with him at the time, were certain of what they had seen. So he returned to the spot during the following morning, when daylight permitted a close investigation of such evidence as the animal's trail. No basis for doubt was left when he found a series of footprints that could have been made by no animal other than a bear. . . .

All who saw the tracks could not remain skeptical of the declaration of Mr. Polson that a bear had at least been present in the region. And much of the former inclination to treat stories of the presence of bears in the Park without much seriousness has turned into a livelier interest in the possibility that these creatures may be present more often than we know.

Park biologists doubt that any bears are permanent residents of the Park. However, black bears or their tracks are seen occasionally within the park boundaries, particularly on the North Rim.

COUGARS ON THE SOUTH RIM OF GRAND CANYON

H.R. Lauzon, Park Ranger
December, 1929.

THE COUGAR WAS FORMERLY a very widely distributed mammal, ranging over practically all of North America as far north as the present Canadian boundary. In various localities throughout the country, representatives of the genus are known as the puma, mountain lion, panther, or painter. Today, it is extinct in a large part of its original range.

The mountain lion, or cougar, of the North Rim of Grand Canyon . . . has long attracted national interest not only because of its former great abundance and consequent depredations on grazing and other animals, but also because it is the largest North American species of cat. It is not generally known, however, that cougars inhabit the South Rim country, yet there have been several killed in that section within recent years. . . .

In early February, 1928, cougar tracks were seen in the snow at a point near Rowe Well, which is about three miles west of Grand Canyon Village. These were reported by Sherman Moore of the local post office. . . .

From the fact that there were more cougar tracks seen in this locality last winter, it is believed that this animal ranged from Rowe Well to the Apache Point country. Undoubtedly, however, there are others scattered about the South Rim country of Grand Canyon, and these play a not unimportant part in the wildlife story of the region.

HUMAN HISTORY

CHAPTER VIII
Archaeology and Ethnobotany

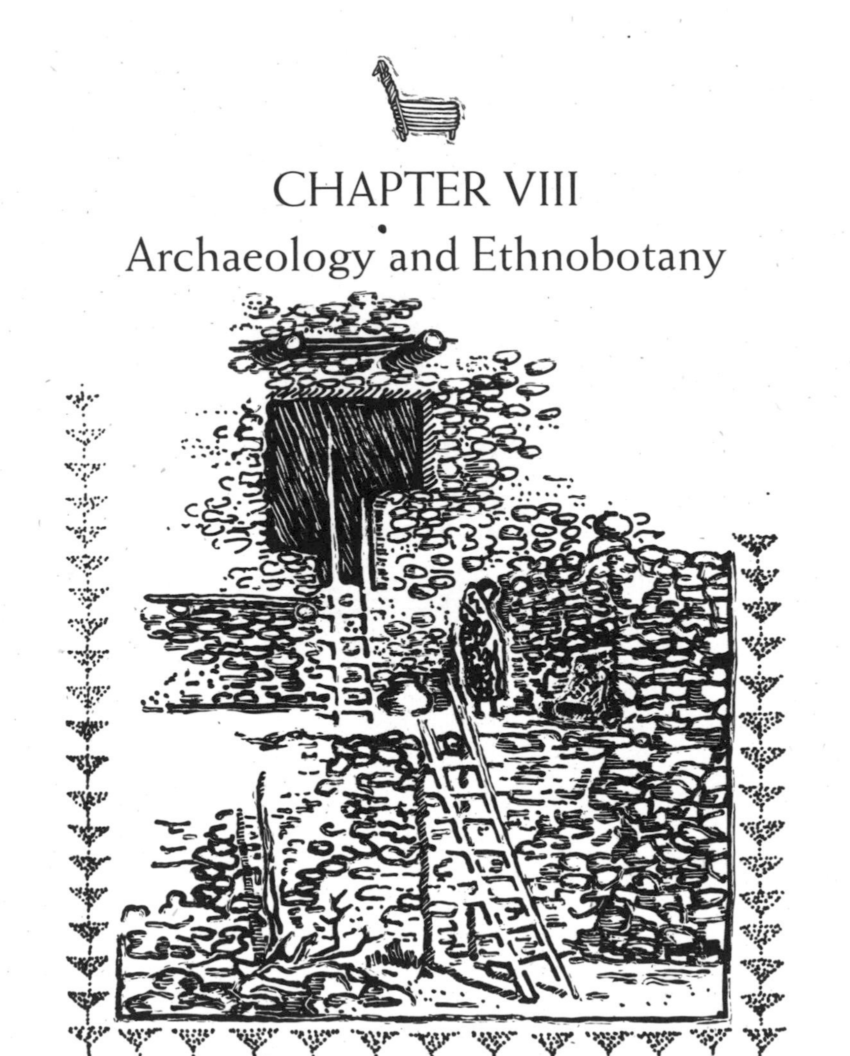

ARCHAEOLOGY

June, 1930.

ARCHAEOLOGICAL WORK in the Grand Canyon region is being carried on this summer by the staff of Gila Pueblo of Globe, Arizona. This is the first work of this kind to be done in the Grand Canyon National Park.

WAYSIDE MUSEUM OF ARCHAEOLOGY EXPEDITION

Harold S. Gladwin, Director of Gila Pueblo
June, 1930.

THE TENTS WERE HARDLY PITCHED before the staff began work on the survey which had been planned. This survey is designed to place the pueblo at Lipan Point, which we have called the Tusayan Ruin, in its proper relation to the surrounding culture. . . .

The method we have followed has been to divide our staff into groups, and allot to each group an area to be surveyed. . . .

When a ruin is found, we collect one hundred fifty fragments of pottery, picking up all the various types; the ruin is given a serial number and is photographed; a description is written giving such details as its location, type, size, number of rooms, condition, masonry, general surroundings, etc.

. . . [W]e have collected over two hundred sites within a radius of twenty-five miles.

NOTELETS

December, 1931.

THREE INTERESTING PUEBLO RUINS were found this past month near the end of the Great Thumb Point in the extreme western part of the Park. They were exceptionally large, one at least being considerably larger than the recently excavated Tusayan ruin. As in the case of most of the ruins in this area, an abundance of potsherds and chipped pieces of chert and obsidian were found in the neighborhood. . . . The pottery fragments suggested that the ruins were of about the same age as those further east (approximately 1200 A.D.)

April, 1931.

THE TUSAYAN RUIN on the South Rim of Grand Canyon, which was partly excavated by the Gila Pueblo staff of Globe, Arizona, this past summer, has been definitely dated by Mr. E.W. Haury of that institution. By the use of tree rings, he determined that it was occupied between 1180 and 1205 A.D. This work was based on results from the examination of six pieces of charcoal—four from "Kiva A" and two from "Kiva B." [A kiva is a ceremonial room.] The accuracy of this dating was confirmed by Dr. A.E. Douglass of the University of Arizona. Mr. Haury also determined that "Kiva B," which is contiguous with the rooms of the dwelling, was built about fifteen years prior to the unattached "Kiva A." The former apparently burned down, necessitating the building of the latter.

Astronomer A.E. Douglass was the father of tree-ring dating, which was a great boon to archaeologists. Noting the relationship of climate to the annual growth rings of trees—wet years produce thick rings and dry years produce thin ones—Douglass realized that he could chart the weather cycles of the past by examining very old wood from ruins. He worked with archaeologists to develop a weather record for the Colorado Plateau by overlapping the "floating chronologies" found in the roof beams of ancient pueblos. When wood providing the final link between the past and the present was discovered in 1928, Douglass had an absolute chronology for the region. Charred fragments from the Tusayan kivas could thus be assigned exact dates.

GRAND CANYON ARCHAEOLOGY

Russell Hastings, Gila Pueblo
June, 1932.

AS MY READERS MAY OR MAY NOT KNOW, the Grand Canyon region falls within the bounds of an area known to archaeologists under the generally accepted term of the Kayenta district, and the culture represented here is a part of the Kayenta culture. In order to get a true conception of the remains to be seen near the Grand Canyon, we must go back into or beyond the beginnings of the Kayenta culture as such.

In the beginning . . . parts of the Southwest were occupied by a people commonly known as "Basketmakers," the name being derived from their greatest cultural expression, basketry . . . whose culture can be divided roughly into three stages. In the first of these (Basketmaker I), the principal occupation was hunting. In the second (Basketmaker II), agriculture was introduced from a source concerning which there is much controversy. . . . In the third (Basketmaker III), pottery was introduced. By this time, the people had developed circular houses of rock slabs, with timber roofs built both in caves and in the open. . . .

Civilization, if the term may be applied to so primitive* a people, was now on a firm agricultural basis, which allowed probably an increase in population and certainly higher developments in the various arts and crafts. Pottery was of a much better character, both in regard to the making and decorating of the pieces. Architecture changed first to rectangular subsurface or pithouses, then to small one- or two-room houses above ground. By this time, a considerable area was covered by these peoples, and the next step was the grouping together of their stone dwellings into loosely-knit colonies. Characteristic advancements in the pottery are our best criteria for this period, the pottery being very well made and decorated with broad lines, the designs geometric and forceful. Of this period more than one hundred sites have been found along the South Rim of the Grand Canyon, and over fifty along the North Rim.

Our next development is evidenced by the building of communal houses, frequently of more than one storey. The Tusayan Ruin at Grand Canyon is of this type. It was excavated by Gila Pueblo in 1930. It was found to contain, on the ground plan, two kivas [ceremonial rooms], four dwelling rooms on the west side, five storage rooms on the north side, and probably the same on the south side, which was left unexcavated in order to show visitors to the ruin in what condition it was before any work had been done. That three of the four rooms in the main (western) block of the ruin were two storeys high is shown by the facts that: in one room seven metates [grinding stones] were found, which is an unreasonable number even if some of them were on the roof; a wall considered to have fallen through from the second storey was found, partly demolished and without foundations, across Room 1; and . . . the fill of the rooms and talus is sufficient to have carried the walls to two storeys in height. . . .

The population of the village, if we can judge from conditions in modern pueblos, would have been about four persons per room, or a maximum population of twenty-eight. Their period of residence is a questionable matter. That it was short is evidenced by the small rubbish mound, the lack of growth by accretion, and the absence of worn-out implements such as metates and manos. . . .

Migrations of primitive peoples are among the greatest problems with which the archaeologist has to deal. Sometimes, the cause can be laid to: change of food supply, climatic change, oppression by hostile neighbors or invaders, or any of a number of similar reasons. . . .

That the present descendants of the Shoshone-Basketmaker complex . . . are the present day Hopis, who live on the mesas in the midst of the Painted Desert, and that the builders of the Tusayan Ruin were a

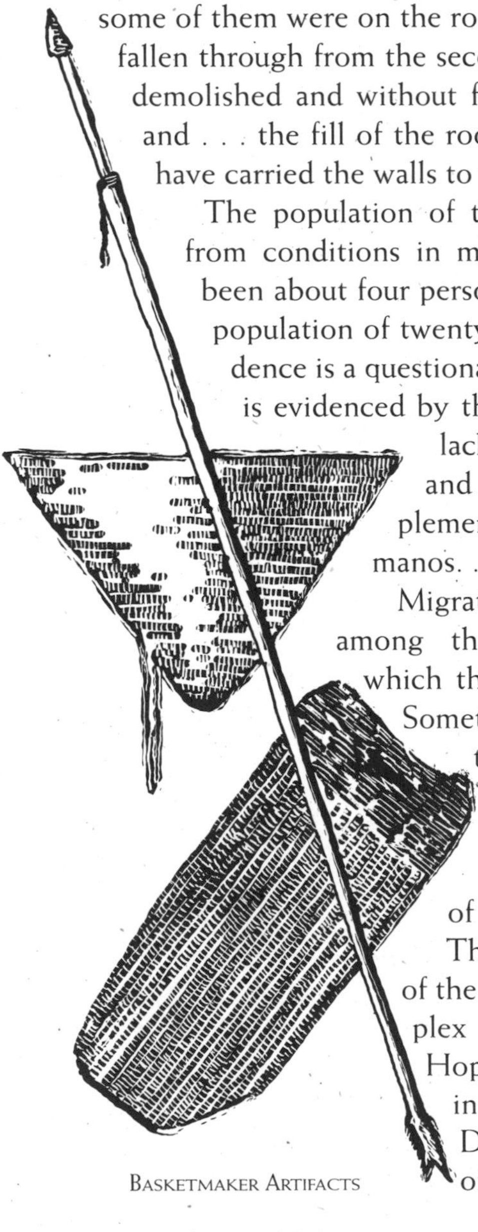

Basketmaker Artifacts

branch of these peoples, is shown conclusively by a series of cultural expressions displaying all the steps and stages of progress from the earliest to the latest. Among these, the pottery series is the most complete and the most convincing.

*Archaeologists today generally avoid value-laden terms such as "primitive." The word can be used to mean "early," or "ancient," but when contrasted with the term "civilization" as it is here, its use suggests a cultural bias on the part of the *primitive* archaeologist.

A LARGE CLIFF DWELLING

Barbara Hastings McKee
October, 1933.

A WEALTH OF MATERIAL indicating the presence of ancient man is to be found not only on the south side of Grand Canyon, but also on the North Rim and in the side canyons to the north of the Colorado River. Most of the ruins north of the river have been seen only infrequently, and by few white men. Most of these men have not been archaeologists, so we have today only vague stories of the things that have been seen and found. The whole area is waiting to be studied.

Not long ago I had the opportunity of visiting Powell Saddle, which connects a plateau of the same name with the main part of the North Rim of Grand Canyon, at a place some 30 miles west of Grand Canyon Lodge. . . . We hiked down a trail from the Canyon rim, and visited a spring of clear water a few hundred feet east of the saddle.

About a hundred yards east of the spring, we came to a flat, wide platform at the base of the Coconino sandstone—the sheer, white cliff of which towered above. On this ledge had once been a settlement, for we could see the outlines of numerous rooms with the stones still built up, and on a large talus slope in front we found fragments of pottery. . . .

Since this ruin was built on a flat, wide ledge so near the water and so accessible to the trail, it has been a favorite camping place for cowboys. Ranger Ed Laws, who has visited the place several times in past years, says that a great deal more of it was standing when he first saw it. A few years ago, a prospector spent the winter near this place and pulled down many of the walls. Moving the flat slabs some hundred feet nearer the spring, he built himself a small house under an overhanging rock. Thus, this prehistoric dwelling has been slowly demolished.

By 1993, about twenty-seven hundred archaeological sites had been recorded at Grand Canyon, of which seventy-five percent date from the pre-European era.

From a superficial examination of stray pottery fragments, or sherds which we picked up, Mr. Louis Schellbach has estimated that this ruin belonged to the last phase of Pueblo II culture, or the first phase of Pueblo III. This dates it roughly as being built and occupied somewhere between 1000 and 1200 A.D.

ANCIENT POTTERY REBUILT

January, 1934.

IN THESE DAYS WHEN Grand Canyon National Park is a beehive of activity at the hands of the Civilian Conservation Corps, National Industrial Recovery Act Workers, and Civil Works Administration Workers, it is worthwhile noting that some of this industry has found its way into the Educational and Research Division. Four of the C.C.C. boys were assigned to museum detail.

Their first job was to assist Ranger Naturalist Louis Schellbach in the reorganization of the archaeological exhibits at Wayside Museum of Archaeology. Part of the work consisted of assembling and restoring a number of ancient Indian pottery specimens. . . .

Many of our readers will find it difficult to realize the amount of careful, painstaking work all this has involved. Add to this the fact that none of these boys had had any previous experience in this kind of work. But a very valuable asset has been their decided interest in this project and their willingness and ability to learn. Such work as these C.C.C. boys are doing can be classed as the highest type of conservation work.

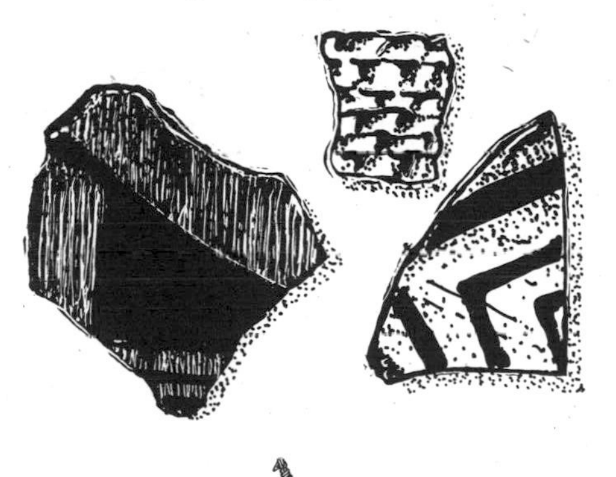

INDIAN USES OF JUNIPER IN THE GRAND CANYON REGION

Donald E. McHenry, Junior Naturalist
April, 1934.

—The Juniper Among Ancient Indians—

FROM THE JUNIPERS and related species found in the outlying parts of the Grand Canyon region come some of the food, clothing, medicine, and ceremonial objects used, not only by the present day Indian, but also by his prehistoric ancestors as well. . . . At the end of the Basketmaker II period, there appeared unfired clay containers, molded in baskets to prevent cracking as the clay dried. A binder of juniper bark was used to further strengthen these containers. At another time, ten juniper bark cradles bound with yucca fibers were found. There are many indications that juniper bark was a very important raw material in the Basketmakers' industry, as it was used in making cradles, sandals, torches, and as padding for bed nets and baby carriers. Sometimes, it was woven into bags.

—The Juniper Among the Modern Indians—

THERE IS A CERTAIN FASCINATION in the archaeology of this region which merges imperceptibly into the customs and traditions of the present-day Indians. Here we find nations with strange manners of living, unfamiliar religious beliefs, and ceremonies which intrigue the imagination. After seeing the unfamiliar and often weird forms of sparse vegetation which cover that area which these people call home, it is hard to believe that these are the things from which the Indians eke out a part of their living.

The Havasupai Indians, a small tribe who dwell near the bottom of Grand Canyon, eat the berries of the Utah juniper as food. . . . These berries are collected after they have fallen to the ground, pulverized in a bedrock mortar, soaked in water, put into the mouth by the handful, and the juice sucked. The solid matter is then spat out. . . . At the Hopi pueblo of Hano, the young people and children eat the berries as a delicacy. They are considered more palatable if heated in an open pan. The Hopis of this same pueblo also chew the gum of the juniper with relish. . . .

Among the Havasupai Indians, a palm drill is sometimes used to kindle a fire using rubbed, dry, juniper bark for tinder. If the reader has ever enjoyed the aroma of burning juniper wood, he will understand one reason why it is the favorite firewood of the Tewa, Zuni, and other Indians of the Southwest. . . . Long shreds of juniper bark, bound compactly with yucca fibers, were formerly used as torches in illuminating the home or in carrying fire from house to house. . . .

Sleeping mats are made from juniper bark by the Havasupais. The bark is pounded until soft and then woven into rectangular mats. The ends are bound by stitching. . . .

A FOOD PLANT OF THE INDIANS

Barbara Hastings, Ranger Naturalist
July, 1929.

FOR UNTOLD AGES, THE MESCAL has been a favorite food of the Indians. When a plant reaches maturity and before it sends up the flowerstalk, they pry it loose from the ground. Rolling it over, spikes down, they slip a pole under each side where it is caught between the leaves, and carry it to their mescal pit. Here they have had a fire burning until the rocks are hot. Dumping the mescal on the hot rocks, they then cover it over with more rocks, and build a fire on top of the pile. It takes about three days and nights to thoroughly cook a mescal. When the rocks are finally thrown to one side, the mescal is found with the inner, meaty core thoroughly cooked, and it is sweet and juicy. The taste resembles that of candied sweet potatoes.

Rocky pits encircled by stones which have been thrown back can be seen in many places in the Grand Canyon today. When they were used or who used them, we cannot always tell, although those on the south side of the Colorado River probably were used by the ancestors of the Havasupai Indians. These Indians today live in one of the large side canyons (Havasu Canyon) of the Grand Canyon, and still cook the mescal in this primitive way.

THE YUCCA: SWORDLIKE YET FRIENDLY

Barbara Hastings McKee
January, 1932.

AS ONE TRAVELS through the arid southwest across our American deserts or semi-deserts, his notice cannot help but be attracted by the yuccas which are very common.

These plants are also called Spanish bayonets, because of their daggerlike leaves of greenish-blue. . . .

Starting with the root, we find where the plant received its common name: soapweed. As far as I can ascertain, all the Indians in New Mexico and Arizona use it for soap, although the narrowleaf yucca is preferred by the Navajos and Hopis for this purpose. Even today with our cheap and good commercial soaps, the Havasupais, Navajos, and Hopis whom I have questioned use the yucca . . . for shampooing their hair. The root of the plant is crushed and bruised, hot water is then poured over it, and a rich lather whipped up. After thoroughly rubbing this lather into the hair, it is rinsed out with clear water and the hair tossed and dried in the sunshine. The soft, shiny tresses of the Indians are a good advertisement for this soap. . . .

The spiked leaves of the *Yucca baccata* are very fibrous. The short ends of the fibers hang from the edges of the leaves, giving them a ragged appearance. From time immemorial, Indians in this part of the country have used these threads for making twine and rope. Before sheep and goats were brought to America by the Spaniards, blankets were sometimes woven of yucca fibers, and strips of rabbit fur were occasionally interwoven with the yucca to make a warmer and more ornamental fabric. The prehistoric inhabitants of this region made sandals of yucca. Even into modern times the Navajos used such footgear, but with the introduction of sheep and goats, these were no longer made, the buckskin shoe seen today taking their place. . . .

A delicacy greatly prized by all Indians in the Southwest is the fruit of the yucca. It is very meaty, and said to be delicious after it has been roasted until the outer skin can be stripped off. It is supposed to taste like a perfectly baked apple. The Zunis in New Mexico make a stiff jelly or conserve by boiling the fruit after it has been well masticated. The resulting, jelly-like mass is formed into pats and dried in the sun. In this way it can be preserved indefinitely. When chunks of this conserve are broken off and soaked in water, the resulting liquid is very sweet. Before the Zuni Indians had sugar, this syrup was used for sweetening. . . .

The *Yucca baccata* as it grows out on the desert is more often than not looked upon with disfavor by the white man. To him, it is just another unlovely plant with sharp, pointed leaves to be avoided. But to natives of the country, it is a beautiful and useful gift of the gods.

SOME GRAND CANYON PLANTS AND THEIR USES

Pauline Mead, Ranger Naturalist
September, 1930.

LOW, SCRUBBY TREES, SHRUBS, AND FLOWERS of the northern semi-desert cover the plateau that lies on the South Rim of the Grand Canyon. It was upon these plants and the native game animals that early Indians and pioneers of the country had to subsist. On first impression, it would seem that such a living might be meager enough. But the pinyon pine, the Spanish bayonet, and the cactus, the century plant, and the cliffrose all contributed leaf, root, stem, and fruit to satisfy the needs of the Indian and the pioneer.

Probably the cactus contributed more and in a greater variety of ways than any other one native plant. It was and still is used as fruit and vegetable . . . and the spines were sometimes used for hooks and awls. . . .

The cactus stem is used as a vegetable. Young, tender pods of the prickly pear are often peeled, cut into strips, and boiled or fried. They taste something like string beans, and are called "nopalillos." Buds of blossoms are frequently cooked in the same way.

The barrel cactus found in the lower parts of the Grand Canyon contains a great deal of water, so is most welcome to a thirsty desert traveler. The Papago Indians, during the dry season, get their water supply from the cactus. The water is

Pinyon Pine

obtained by cutting a slice off the top of the plant, mashing the flesh into a pulp, and squeezing out the water. The water tastes rather salty and herbaceous, but is not unpleasant. It is used by the Indians as a flavoring in cooking, and is often mixed with bread dough.

Cactus seeds, because of their oily content, are ground up and used as butter on tortillas by the Indians. Sometimes, the seeds are parched and ground into a meal. . . .

The pinyon pine with its rich nut, and the Utah juniper with its oily berry, have much to offer. The pinyon nut, borne in baskets at the base of the cone scale, is sometimes ground by the Navajos and used as a butter spread, since it contains a high percentage of fat. It is also roasted and ground into a meal. The Hopis use the nut as a shortening in cakes, and to enrich stews. . . .

Brigham Tea

The cliffrose or buckbrush is sometimes called "quinine bush." If tea is made from the leaves it may be used as quinine. . . .

Brigham tea (*Ephedra*) makes an excellent tea by steeping the branches. . . .

A wild tobacco grows quite abundantly on both North and South Rims of Grand Canyon. Its leaves are dried and smoked by the Hopi and Navajo Indians. Before the rain ceremonies in the late summer, these Indians smoke this tobacco and blow it in the four directions.

Both the Navajos and Hopis are practical botanists. The Navajo plant names show the result of careful observation. The names are descriptive of roots, leaves, flowers, and the uses of the plant.

For example, the Navajo name for dock is *Ch'il bikétł' óól łitsooígíí*, which means "plant with yellow root." Yarrow is called *Hazéíyiltsee'í* ("chipmunk-like tail") for its long fluffy leaves, while *Tł'éé' íigahiits'óóz*—"white at night"—is Navajo for evening primrose. Cliffrose is *Awééts'áál*, or "baby cradle," because its shredded, absorbent bark was once used to line cradleboards. The horsetail, a natural sandpaper, is known as *Ałtį́į' jik'aashí*: "bow smoother."

CHAPTER IX
History

The Grand Canyon from Yaki Point.

THE NAMING OF THE GRAND CANYON

Barbara Hastings McKee
November, 1933.

THE GRAND CANYON WAS FIRST seen by white men in 1540, when a scouting party in [the] charge of Don Garcia Lopez de Cardenas was sent out by Coronado from the Indian village of Zuni. However, they seem to have left the great chasm unnamed. Cardenas realized that the river at the bottom was one that had already been discovered and crossed by Melchior Diaz, then named the Tison (Firebrand) River, but he did not refer to the Canyon by any name.

In 1858, Lieutenant J.C. Ives and J.S. Newberry, geologist, having completed a survey of the Lower Colorado River, visited this huge gorge and wrote of it under the names of "Big Canon" and "Great Canon." It is interesting to note what Ives had to say about this country: "The region last explored is, of course, altogether valueless. It can be approached only from the south, and after entering it there is nothing to do but leave. . . ." [Also see the comments of Lieutenant Ives under *The Explorer*, pages 35–36.]

It was only a few years later, however, in 1869 that Major John Wesley Powell explored the length of the Green and Colorado Rivers. He passed through the great canyon in the course of the journey, and it was he who gave it the name Grand Canyon, probably shortly after this trip. Mr. Frederick S. Dellenbaugh, who was one of Major Powell's topographers on his second trip in 1871 and 1872, tells how Powell used that name in his report following the journey, and how it was not until his topographers made the first preliminary map of the region in the winter of 1872 and 1873 that the name was recorded on a map.

THE CORONADO EXPEDITION

Stephen B. Jones, Ranger Naturalist
June, 1929.

A NUMBER OF PLACE NAMES in the Grand Canyon have been bestowed in memory of Coronado's expedition. First, Coronado himself is commemorated by a butte near Grandview Point. Cardenas Butte records the name of his lieutenant, who actually discovered the Canyon. Tovar Terrace (and the name "El Tovar") commemorate Pedro de Tovar, who was the first to learn of the existence of the Canyon from the Hopi Indians.

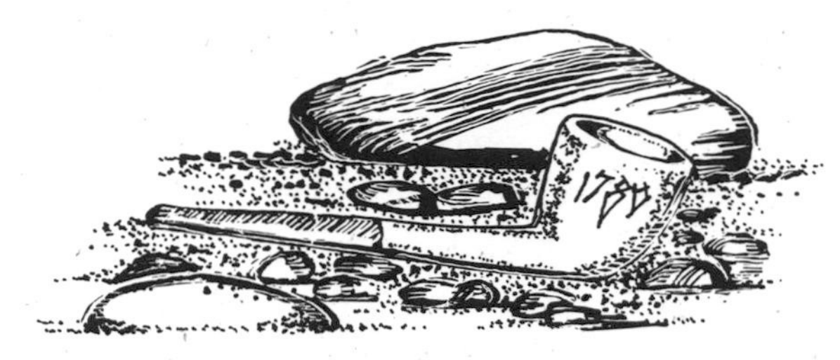

HOW PIPE CREEK RECEIVED ITS NAME

Hugh H. Waesche, Ranger Naturalist
June, 1933.

SOME OF THE EARLY PIONEERS in Grand Canyon were certain that such a wonderful natural phenomenon as the Canyon must contain vast riches in valuable ores, so much prospecting for gold, copper, lead, and zinc was a natural result. The large number of prospect holes to be found at several localities along the Canyon walls is mute evidence of their activities. These men often traveled along the Tonto Platform, which was the only practical way to follow the course of the Colorado without resorting to the plateaus along the rims. Good showings of copper were discovered in the Redwall limestone near Grandview. Considerable prospecting was done at a locality near what is now known as the "Corkscrew," on Bright Angel Trail.

One day in 1894, four of these hardy prospectors came along the Tonto Trail from Grandview, headed for the "Corkscrew" locality. . . . R.H. Cameron, for some reason, went on ahead of the other members of the party. When he reached the point where the stream now known as "Pipe Creek" is located, he discovered an old, meerschaum pipe lying on the ground. He picked up the pipe and scratched on it a date of about one hundred years previous, then placed it on a willow twig in such a way that the members of the party following could not miss it as they came by. His little joke worked perfectly, since the three others discovered the pipe when they came along. One can well imagine the speculation as to how the pipe got there and what the fate of the original owner might have been. It seemed evident that there had been some traveler along that very route many years before. Cameron enjoyed the joke by himself for awhile but it was too good to keep, so the story finally leaked out. It was this little incident which was responsible for the name Pipe Creek, which the stream continues to bear.

Pipe Creek flows into the Colorado from the south side of the Grand Canyon, nearly opposite Bright Angel Creek. It may be seen from the Yavapai Observation Station as the canyon directly below and to the right—the next tributary canyon east of the one containing Garden Creek.

HISTORY NOTE

Edwin D. McKee, Park Naturalist
September, 1934.

A "CLIFF-DWELLING," which has obviously been made by man of post-Columbian times at the isolated junction of the main and Little Colorado Rivers, was reported a few years ago by Mr. Emery Kolb of Grand Canyon. While making geological studies in the area this past year, the writer was able to relocate this interesting site. . . . Built beneath the cliff of Tapeats sandstone southeast of the confluence of the rivers, this structure was both well-concealed and well-protected from the elements. Who built it and when are the questions that cannot be answered, but the small iron plow . . . testifies to the probable intentions of some pioneer to plow the Little Colorado River delta. Only those who are acquainted with the extreme solitude and isolation of the locality, and the difficulties of access to it, can truly appreciate the hermit-like qualities of any man who sought existence in such a place.

Major John Wesley Powell also made note of this structure on his first voyage in 1869, but at that time it was still clearly a Pueblo ruin. In 1890, a prospector named Ben Beamer modified the ruin and lived in it while he searched for minerals in the area. The plow is evidence of Beamer's efforts to support himself, but he had little success at either prospecting or farming.

YAVAPAI OBSERVATION STATION

P.P. Patraw, Assistant Superintendent
March, 1930.

THE PURPOSE OF THE YAVAPAI Observation Station is, as its name implies, to serve as an observatory from which may be seen the things that tell the story of the formation, birth, and growth of the Grand Canyon. The Grand Canyon is the one great exhibit. Mineral, fossil, and other specimens are placed in the building, but not as museum specimens; rather, they act as assistants in the interpretation and recitation of the story.

After an exhaustive study made by Doctor John C. Merriam, Chairman of the National Park Service educational committee, and his associates, Yavapai Point was selected as the site best adapted to the purpose. The site is ideal from all standpoints. From it may be plainly viewed the five great features of the story: erosion, deposition, crustal movement, ancient life, and modern life. There is the Colorado River, the power that cut and carried away the materials leaving the great void called the Grand Canyon, still alive and carrying on its work, which will not be completed until the mass within its ultimate reach is once more at sea level. A sandbar may be seen, deposited from the river, and telling a story today in the same words in which the story of the building of the strata composing the walls of the Canyon was told. There is the great Bright Angel Fault, telling of crustal movement which to a much greater extent is depicted in the walls of the Canyon, once beneath the level of the sea. There are the places in which the fossil remains of paleozoic life are found, telling of the development of life existing at the time the walls were formed. There is the wide range of modern life zones, varying from the Lower Sonoran at the bottom to the Canadian at the rim. Thus, we see movement in apparent stability, youth and age, side by side.

THE REFERENCE LIBRARY

May, 1930.

THE ESTABLISHMENT OF A MUCH-NEEDED reference library at Grand Canyon has been started in earnest this season. This library is to contain literature dealing with various scientific subjects, natural history, history, and the Grand Canyon region in general. It is hoped that in time, a complete collection of all literature dealing with this region will be obtained. The library is located in the Naturalist's office at the Park Service administration building, and now contains two hundred seventy volumes. These were obtained entirely though the generous contributions of interested private individuals and of various scientific institutions. The Carnegie Institution, the Smithsonian Institution, the U.S. Geological Survey, and the U.S. Biological Survey have been especially helpful in this work.

THE GRAND CANYON NATURAL HISTORY ASSOCIATION

PURPOSES

1. To stimulate and encourage scientific research and investigation in the fields of geology, botany, zoology, ethnology, archaeology, and related subjects in the Grand Canyon region.

2. To assist:
   (a) in the establishment of a natural history museum;
   (b) in the further development of the Yavapai Station and the Wayside Museum of Archaeology;
   (c) in the preparation of exhibits and other projects for the interpretation of the natural features of the region.

3. To keep the association members informed regarding research and educational activities, and wildlife observations in the Grand Canyon region.

4. To publish, in cooperation with the National Park Service, "Grand Canyon Nature Notes," which will appear monthly throughout the year. It is planned to have these printed by the Association.

5. To publish, in cooperation with the National Park Service, "Technical Bulletins" dealing with the various fields of natural science represented in the region.

6. To build up and maintain the Grand Canyon Reference Library—an institution available to all students and others interested.

The operations, business, property, and assets of the Association shall be strictly limited to purposes which shall be scientific and educational, in order that the Association shall not be constituted nor operated for profit, and so that no part of the net income of the Association shall inure to the benefit of any member.

A NATIONAL PARK CREED

John C. Merriam, President
Carnegie Institution of Washington
December, 1926.

WHILE THE NATIONAL PARKS SERVE in an important sense as recreation areas, their primary uses extend far into that fundamental education which concerns real appreciation of nature. Here, beauty in its truest sense receives expression, and exerts its influence along with recreation and formal education. To me, the parks are not merely places to rest and exercise and learn. They are regions where one looks through the veil to meet the realities of nature, and the unfathomable power behind it.

SUGGESTED READING

For an up-to-date appreciation of Grand Canyon's natural and human history, the following books are recommended:

GENERAL

Grand Canyon National Park by Jeremy Schmidt. 1993, Houghton Mifflin Company, New York.

EARTH SCIENCE

Introduction to Grand Canyon Geology by Michael Collier. 1980, Grand Canyon Natural History Association.

Grand Canyon Geology edited by Stanley S. Beus and Michael Morales. 1993, Oxford University Press and Museum of Northern Arizona.

LIFE SCIENCE

The Colorado River Through Grand Canyon by Steven W. Carothers and Bryan T. Brown. 1991, University of Arizona Press, Tucson.

ARCHAEOLOGY

Sketch of Grand Canyon Prehistory by A. Trinkle Jones and Robert Euler. 1979, Grand Canyon Natural History Association.

HISTORY

In the House of Stone and Light by J. Donald Hughes. 1978, Grand Canyon Natural History Association.

All of these books are available through the Grand Canyon Natural History Association, Post Office Box 399, Grand Canyon, AZ 86023.

The End